Penn State Football

Also in the Sports by the Numbers™ series:

Penn State Football

An *Interactive* Guide to the World of Sports

SB

Savas Beatie

New York and California

Printed in the United States of America

Cataloging-in-Publication Data is available from the Library of Congress.

ISBN13: 978-1-932714-52-4

10 09 08 07 06 05 04 03 02 01
First edition, first printing

SB

Published by
Savas Beatie LLC
521 Fifth Avenue, Suite 1700
New York, NY 10175
Phone: 610-853-9131

Editorial Offices:

Savas Beatie LLC
P.O. Box 4527
El Dorado Hills, CA 95762
Phone: 916-941-6896
(E-mail) editorial@savasbeatie.com

Savas Beatie titles are available at special discounts for bulk purchases in the United States by corporations, institutions, and other organizations. For more details, please contact Special Sales, P.O. Box 4527, El Dorado Hills, CA 95762. You may also e-mail us at sales@savasbeatie.com, or click over for a visit to our website at www.savasbeatie.com for additional information.

For the Glory. For the Kids.
WE ARE . . . PENN STATE!

Contents

Foreword

One.

Sorry, Three Dog Night, but in this Penn State book, one is hardly the loneliest number. And we are not just talking about No. 1. Or Number One. Or #1. Although Penn State football has been there, done that, too. Two, actually:

National champion, college football, 1982.

National champion, college football, 1986.

For the Nittany Lions, those number ones were not the destination. They were just monuments along the journey. It is the road less traveled in college football that really matters.

Discipline. Humility. Sportsmanship. Scholarship. Community. They all matter.

So while the Nittany Lions may be successful, they'll never be flashy. No logo on the helmet or names on the jerseys. Black shoes, white hats, no stickers for doing what you're supposed to do. Players who go to class and graduate. A coach who wears a tie to work and scolds errant players, referees, newspapermen, and wayward drivers alike.

That plays well in Pennsylvania with Pennsylvanians. It did when Joe Paterno succeeded his boss, Rip Engle, as head coach in 1966 and it does to this very day. We really are a blue-collar state, still. Pennsylvania Dutch (a derivation of the German deutsche) are strong, stubborn, and honest. Steel, coal, and manure are on our hands and in our blood. We have a grimy work ethic, live our values, and are grateful for education. College remains the way out of the mines of Scranton, the steel mills of Pittsburgh, the farms of Manheim, and the small villes of Route 6. Right now, three out of ten students who enroll at Penn State are the first generation of their families to attend college. Ever. The American dream still lives. At Penn State and on the football field.

That is by design, thanks in part to Abe Lincoln. Penn State's roots date back to 1855, when it was founded as an agricultural college. Its soul was cemented in 1862 when Lincoln signed the Land Grant Act, which pledged that higher education would be within the reach of Americans of average means while serving the public good. Nearly a century-and-a-half later, the character remains.

The result is an alumni base that appreciates the education it received and the football team that represents it. All for one and one for football.

For over a decade, Penn State has annually drawn over a million fans on the road and at home in Beaver Stadium. Until Michigan completes its renovations, Beaver Stadium has more seats than any other college football stadium in the country, with its 107,282 seats—1,081 more than Michigan has. The Beav has to be that big to hold so many Penn Staters. There are a lot of us, you know:

- It has been reported that more high school students submit their SAT scores to Penn State than any other institution of higher learning.
- The Penn State Alumni Association is the largest dues-paying alumni group in the United States, with 160,742 members.
- Penn State ranks first among living alumni, with over 440,000.

Here's a number that says all you need to know about Penn State students: $7,490,114.87. That's how much Penn State undergraduates raised for children with cancer in 2009 with its annual THON dance marathon, the most successful philanthropic effort in the country.

Penn Staters are proud of their football. But even prouder of how Joe Paterno has built the empire the right way. Not cheating, no NCAA violations, honest work in the classroom.

Sure, Joe's teams have delivered victories by the basketful. Entering the 2009 season, Joe ranked No. 1 — there's that number again — on the Division I college football all-time victory list, with 383 wins. But given that Penn State is first and foremost an academic institution, the numbers Paterno's student-athletes have amassed in the classroom are even more impressive.

In the fall of 2008, a program record 55 football players earned a GPA of at least 3.0. And of that group, a record 19 made Dean's List recognition with a GPA of 3.5 or higher. Since 1966, Penn State has had 15 Hall of Fame Scholar-Athletes, 31 first-team Academic All-Americans and 18 NCAA Postgraduate Scholarship winners. The Nittany Lions aren't coasting on past success, either. Penn State has had at least one Academic All-American in each of the past seven seasons.

"The purpose of college football is to serve education," Paterno once said, "not the other way around."

At Penn State, football is an education. And not just for its players, either.

Mike Poorman
Senior Penn State Lecturer & Director of Alumni Relations

Preface

*I*nformation gathered in game programs and yearbooks link generations of Nittany Lions.

An in-depth look at the history of a successful football program isn't just about numbers. Yes, the Sports by the Numbers™ series is based on a strong foundation of numerical greatness, but this book takes that framework and builds a house full of life, color, and everlasting memories.

The numbers may not be the story. But—in pigskin terms—they are the lead blocker paving the way for tales of great players, great teams, and great games.

Michael Poorman gave you a taste of Penn State history in the foreword and the pages that follow are packed with nostalgia from the program's birth in 1887 to Joe Paterno's 43rd season as head coach in 2008.

Perhaps the number that frames Penn State Football best is 121; that equals the number of years for Penn State's proud football history as told through memories and experiences—and framed by numbers.

While the book goes into great detail about Heisman Trophy winner John Cappelletti and NFL Hall of Fame members Jack Ham, Franco Harris, and Lenny Moore, each entry in this Sports by the Numbers™

title is reserved for the Penn State experience—a close family friend to triumph on the Beaver Stadium turf.

No college football fan can truly embrace a program's greatness until he or she lives, no matter how briefly, through the story's setting.

This book provides endless opportunities to pinpoint numbers and discuss their place in Nittany Lion lore. Yet, the significance of each number will hold even more appreciation with a mental picture of the many characters who spend each Saturday cheering on their Nittany Lions.

It's a picture painted on the fertile Central Pennsylvania soil, but one that will forever remain engrained in the minds of a Penn State nation that branches out far beyond Happy Valley's borders.

*   *   *

The doors to Penn State, one of college football's landmark programs, are always open—airing in the permeating stench of rolling farmland and an equally potent whiff of excellence. It was, after all, a true cow college.

Beaver Stadium serves as not just a sporting venue, but as a tourist attraction for those traveling to Pittsburgh or Philadelphia, and a historical monument for the university and its neighboring towns.

Football, family, and a college student's first taste of freedom make for an interesting dynamic between the townies of State College and their 42,000 next-door neighbors in University Park.

The borough closely resembles a Norman Rockwell painting of small town USA. Stone houses—some of them ordered in the Sears catalog generations ago—line streets dotted with shade trees. Bookstores, pizza parlors, bars, and souvenir shops cater to students and returning alumni alike. The lifeblood of the town sits in an area that includes the State College High School football stadium, a breeding ground for family bonding and future Nittany Lions.

College Avenue serves as the boundary between adults and adolescents. On any morning, the street is crowded with families and frat brothers, all shopping, eating, and preparing for the day ahead.

Yet, up over the slight hill leading to the campus core lays an alluring life of luxury. Granted, it's spent in a rundown dorm or apartment with Ramen Noodles stocking the cupboard and Natty Ice filling the fridge. But it is Penn State, where many students take more pride in Playboy's party school rankings than they do in impressive GPAs.

The two opposite sides of reality coexist behind an undying love of Nittany Lion football.

"WE ARE . . . PENN STATE."

And that phrase isn't lip service or an advertising slogan generated to increase college applications and season ticket sales. It's real—born straight from a football program built on the ideals of its legendary head coach.

Joe Paterno's inherent beliefs rooted in old school values mark everything from Penn State's touchdown celebrations to its uniforms.

Even at his age and income level, Paterno still lives now where he did 40 years ago, in a modest house situated in a quiet neighborhood six blocks from campus. Up until his leg injury suffered in a sideline collision during the 2006 season, he occasionally walked to work, waving to everyone from the postman to the freshman chemistry major along the way.

Just think about that for a second. The winningest coach in college football history—a man who basically funded an entire library and can order an ice cream (Peachy Paterno) that bears his name—walked to work.

That humility is what keeps him and his football team grounded. A challenging schedule, a national media presence, and suffocating expectations can inflate a man's ego. Just like a high national ranking, 24/7 exposure, and enormous popularity can push a player onto a pedestal.

While each happens on occasion, Paterno's tenure can be summarized by one of his most famous quotes.

"Believe deep down in your heart that you are destined to do great things."

Joe Pa and his players have succeeded in that mission since he took over prior to the 1966 season. National championships, conference crowns, a Heisman Trophy, and cherished records—all achieved the Penn State way.

Yet, achievements are broad strokes in a masterpiece fully realized through the experience.

That experience begins each football weekend at The Corner Room, where weekend breakfasts are served buffet style with a side of Penn

State passion in the form of collectible buttons. After a meal consisting of bacon, eggs, and one of the Ye Olde College Diner's famous sticky buns, you can walk off the calories with a trip to Family Clothesline, where blue and white apparel can be bought in bulk.

Then, adults and students join together in the grass fields surrounding the stadium for a true pigskin tailgate of pork and Pabst Blue Ribbon. On the way to Lot A, travelers will pass Paternoville, a village of tents situated just outside the pearly gates of Paterno's palace. Here, students eat, sleep, and perhaps even study in the days leading up to the big game.

Soaking in the entire pre-kickoff experience makes visitors appreciate what happens inside the stadium even more. The people in the stands care just as much as those on the field.

It's a remarkable feeling of family. Beaver Stadium is never truly closed to a fellow Nittany Lion.

The doors are always open.

Acknowledgments

One wonders where motivation comes from. It sprouts from inner beliefs and convictions, but blossoms behind the love and support of the very people mentioned in this section.

As a student at Penn State, I took ownership in my football team. I had class with All-Big Ten stars and ate lunch across from a Heisman Trophy finalist. I rubbed elbows with a legendary head coach and worshiped the ground he walked on each fall Saturday.

Those brushes with icons have helped me appreciate Penn State's proud football legacy, but as a writer, family and friends have been a bigger part of this project than those scoring touchdowns.

To the people who have been there to see me through the tough times and take part in the good times, I thank you. I thank my parents, who have always stood by me with a blinded faith in my writing ability. They have always been there, and always will be. They have embraced my shortcomings and shown constant love. I couldn't ask for more supportive, more loving parents.

Mom and Dad—I love you.

To my brother, Nate, who one day will be a hot-shot lawyer with a big house, and more importantly in his eyes, a big boat. He and I disagree on college basketball favorites, but we share a common love for Penn State football. Thanks for always being there. Love you bro.

Each person has an inspiration. The person who can yell at you and hug you in a matter of five minutes. The person whose truth is always based in their spirit. The girl I thought I'd never meet.

Tina Marie Gajda doesn't even like Penn State football (most Rutgers graduates are still bitter about the endless beat downs of years past)—but she will read the book—then tell me how much better Ray Rice is than any Nittany Lion running back.

There is no hesitation in my voice. No backspace in my heart. I love you.

My family is a mixed bag of personalities with one very strong common characteristic: love. To Gram and Pap in the Windy City; Gram Rose; Uncle Steve; Aunt Kristy and Bryan; Aunt Cindy; Aunt Missy; Aunt Pauline; Aunt Lisa and Aunt Mary; my godparents Norton and Nancy; and my cousins Carly, Jake, Jonah, Jacy, and Tyler: I love you all and thank you for always being there.

I also need to thank those who will be reading this book from heaven: John Burdinsky (Uncle T); Uncle Frank; Gram and Pap Trexler; Pap Willy; Great Gram Stevens; and Uncle Bill. You all are co-authors in my life. I love you.

Thank you to the good friends who have been a part of my life at one time or another: Andrew Rickert, Ivan Baumwell, James Weldon, Ryan Fortese, Maggie Muklewicz, Jennifer Benner, Ivy Lane, Jennifer Deen, Eric Reimer, John Shapiro, and Veronica Gajda.

In a way, each of you has been a vital part of the supporting cast. Thank you.

To co-authors Marc Maxwell, Daniel Brush, and David Horne, thank you for affording me the opportunity to live out a dream. To Savas Beatie, thank you for your faith in this project and the resources to pull it all together.

Special thanks to Mike Poorman, an excellent professor and an even more talented writer. Mike refined my rough edges to the best of his ability (so blame the poor grammar and syntax on him) and he took the time to write a wonderful foreword.

Also, thanks to the voice of Penn State football Steve Jones, whose knowledge of the sport has been an asset since I started listening to the radio broadcasts. Steve also served as a mentor and a teacher, and for that I'm thankful.

And with one last deep breath, we almost reach the end. These people have also impacted my life or this book in one way or another, and to them I say thank you: Penn State professor John Curley; my understanding bosses and co-workers at GSI Interactive, Greg Hartman, Troy Ruch, and Ridge Hughes.

This book isn't for the name on the front of the cover. It is for all of you.

Jared Trexler
June 1, 2009

The Locker

*W*elcome to Sports by the Numbers™ and our Interactive Guide to the World of Sports. In compiling our first 1,000 numbers that we used to tell stories in our debut title, *University of Oklahoma Football*, it was apparent to us that for one reason or another some of the numbers resonated more deeply with us than did others—they were special.

The numbers were all great, but there were some numbers that we were drawn towards and felt the need to expand on more than the others. Our website provided us with the opportunity to do just that in an area we call The Locker.

The team of authors for this title on Penn State Football has used special logos to designate five Hall of Fame numbers and ten All-Star numbers that you will come across as you read the stories that unfold within these pages.

Numbers designated as Hall of Fame or All-Star lets you know that they are among our favorites from this book—and once in the locker room, you will find out why.

Our website is: www.SportsByTheNumbers.com

Use the tab at the top of our homepage or the locker on the bottom right-hand corner of our homepage to enter our locker. Once there you will see the covers of all the SBTN titles that are currently available.

Click on the cover of your favorite SBTN title to view the Hall of Fame and All-Star numbers that the SBTN authors have selected for that book.

You can then click on any number in the locker room to gain access to additional information that may come in the form of pictures, video, audio, text, or random musings from one of the SBTN authors, but regardless, it will enhance the story told by the number, and it will let you know why we feel the number is so significant.

Creating an Interactive World of Sports that combines the best of the traditional book world with the unlimited potential of the Internet is an exciting and fluid process—and we are constantly working on new and better ways to bring together the book world and the cyber world with one goal in mind, to give sports fans the ultimate experience when it comes to reminiscing about their favorite numbers, players, teams, and memories.

Enjoy the experience.

WE ARE . . . PENN STATE!

Fiesta Bowl, January 2, 1987

Miami (Fla.)	0	7	0	3 - 10
Penn State	0	7	0	7 - 14

Scoring

....

Miami - Bratton, 1, run (Cox kick); PSU - Shaffer, 4, run (Manca, kick);
Miami - Seelig, 38, field goal; PSU - Dozier, 6, run (Manca, kick).

Team Statistics	PSU	MIAMI
First Downs	8	22
Total Net Yards	162	445
Net Yards Rushing	109	160
Net Yards Passing	53	285
Passes (Att-Comp-Int)	16-5-1	50-26-5
Punts-Average	9-43.4	4-46.0
Fumbles-Fumbles Lost	5-2	4-2
Penalties-Yards	4-39	9-62

Individual Statistics

....

Rushing
PSU - Dozier 20 for 99, 1 TD; Manoa 8 for 36;
Smith 4 for 13; Roundtree 1 for 3; Thomas 1 for (-3);
Shaffer 9 for (-39), 1 TD.
MIAMI - Highsmith 18 for 119; Bratton 11 for 31, 1 TD;
Williams 5 for 20; Testaverde 9 for (-10).

Passing
PSU - Shaffer 5 for 16, 53 yds., 1 Int.
MIAMI - Testaverde 26 for 50, 285 yds., 5 Int.

Receiving
PSU - Dozier 2 for 12; Hamilton 1 for 23;
Manoa 1 for 12; Siverling 1 for 6.
MIAMI - Blades 5 for 81; Irvin 5 for 55; Perriman 4 for 37;
Highsmith 3 for 33; Bratton 3 for 32; Henry 3 for 24;
Williams 2 for 20; Roberts 1 for 3.

Attendance: 73,098

"We were a team that couldn't be intimidated, and that's what Miami liked to do to other players. How are you going to intimidate a bunch of steel-town kids from Pittsburgh, Ohio, Pennsylvania? You just can't do that."

— *Penn State linebacker Pete Giftopoulos to BCSfootball.com in 2002*

Chapter One

The Night Penn State Won The War

With the 1986 Orange Bowl loss to Oklahoma still fresh in its minds, Penn State undoubtedly would have played the 1987 Fiesta Bowl on concrete in head coach Joe Paterno's hometown of Brooklyn.

At least that's what Paterno told Fiesta Bowl selection committee chairman Don Myers.

Of course the game was played on grass, although many sportswriters predicted Penn State's chances would have been better on the moon, or perhaps in a cow pasture somewhere out near Bellefonte.

Miami had the Heisman Trophy quarterback, the stylish head coach with a head full of hair spray and an attitude full of moxie, and the South Beach attitude—Cadillac cruisers and party hoppers—followed a group of trendsetters.

The Hurricanes dared to be different, and 20 years later, that collective persona may have been embraced as "hopeful change," but when up against Penn State, it was perceived as adolescent mockery.

Penn State had an executive running its offense—a quarterback named John Shaffer who managed the unit's assets, then eventually oversaw Merrill Lynch's prized funds as his opposing signal-caller, Vinny Testaverde, made a name for himself in the NFL.

Paterno rolled up his pants, wore Coke bottle glasses and used "yesterday speak"—referring back to simpler times and preaching family values. Penn State didn't want to reinvent life's wheel, but rather follow the prodigious spokes of successes past.

The game was dubbed good versus evil. It truly was a clashing of cultures, a perception that pitted the eclectic rebels against the passive Puritans.

It irked Penn State's players, along with the fact that few gave them a chance of pulling the upset and winning the program's second national championship of the decade.

Few, that is, except fellow teammates and coaches, feeding off the underdog role and the extra motivation from events preceding January 2, 1987.

The contest became a spectacle of Super Bowl proportions during a steak fry.

Prior to the planned event, the Hurricanes made news for arriving in Tempe wearing combat fatigues. Writers immediately called Miami's real-life Halloween garb eerily realistic, as the brash Hurricanes had already stated their intentions of a slaughter.

The days leading up to kickoff were filled with media-driven jabs and motivational mind games. It reached a crescendo during skits at the steak fry, beginning with some digs by Penn State punter John Bruno.

Hurricanes defensive tackle Jerome Brown then stood from his seat—an enormous, overpowering figure who looked every bit the villain. He unzipped his sweat suit to again reveal the combat fatigues. "Did the Japanese sit down and eat with Pearl Harbor before they bombed them?" Brown bellowed. "No. We're outta here."

As the Hurricanes marched out of the dining hall, Bruno again rose and rhetorically asked, "Excuse me, but didn't the Japanese lose that war?"

Game on.

And if a game was played on a stat sheet, the above tutorial in history would have little to no relevance today. Miami gained 445 yards by doing—as it thought, and said publicly, all week—anything it wanted between the 20s. Penn State, on the other hand, couldn't throw or even muster a ground game behind D.J. Dozier, accumulating just over one-third of Miami's total offense with 162 yards.

The game took on each team's personality—Miami with glitz, glamour, and offense; Penn State with resolve, defense, and special teams.

And yet, Paterno was strangely at ease. He knew every fable in the book. Tortoise beats the hare, slow and steady wins the race. He instructed his offense to play it safe, Bruno continually punted Miami's offense into a corner, and the Hurricanes constantly coughed up the football.

Three times Testaverde threw the pigskin to a Nittany Lion defender in the first three quarters, yet Miami still had a 10-7 lead with 11:49 left in the game. Penn State's pass defense continued to perplex the star quarterback, and linebacker Shane Conlan intercepted his second pass of the game later in the period.

Dozier capitalized with a touchdown and a prayer, probably figuring the last several minutes would only pass quickly with the grace of God.

Miami found life on its final possession, moving to the Nittany Lions four-yard line before Tim Johnson sacked Testaverde. After an incomplete pass, and with the final pivotal play of the 1987 Fiesta Bowl forthcoming, more than 70 million viewers at home and fans of both sides held their collective breath.

And with Pete Giftopoulos' interception, the Nittany Lion nation exhaled. Defensive coordinator Jerry Sandusky cried, and Joe Paterno won his second national championship in five seasons.

The Hurricanes had dressed for war, but never truly prepared for one.

Giftopoulos' interception sealed a remarkable upset and etched his name and number in Penn State lore.

A number signifying family (1) — each autumn Saturday, the Penn State fraternity joins hands in Beaver Stadium to a deafening chorus in the background: "WE ARE . . . PENN STATE!"

The number of times (2) Penn State carried Joe Paterno off the field as a national champion. The 1982 Nittany Lions beat five teams in the Top 13 of the rankings at the time of the contest. The 1986 season came and went without a blemish—a 12-0 mark realized with 14-10 victory over heavily favored Miami in the Fiesta Bowl.

The number of safeties (3) defensive end Mike Reid caused in a 15-7 victory over Maryland in 1966. The three safeties gave Reid the single game, single season, and career safeties mark.

The single game interception record (4) set by Mike Smith against Ohio University in 1970. Smith's four interceptions led the Nittany Lions past the Bobcats, 32-22.

The number of interceptions (5) Vinny Testaverde threw against a swarming Nittany Lions defense in the 1987 Fiesta Bowl. The Hurricanes signal-caller entered the game with a Heisman Trophy and plenty of confidence, but left the field defeated following his final fatal throw into the hands of Penn State linebacker Pete Giftopoulos near the Nittany Lions end zone in the waning seconds.

The number of yards (6) that stood between All-American running back D.J. Dozier and a national championship. Dozier made his way through the vaunted Miami Hurricane's defense and into the end zone for the eventual championship-clinching touchdown in the 1987 Fiesta Bowl. Dozier ran for 811 yards during the season, becoming the first Nittany Lion to lead the team in rushing four consecutive seasons.

The number of yards (7) Miami quarterback Vinny Testaverde lost on Tim Johnson's sack at the Penn State 13 yard line in the final minute of the 1987 Fiesta Bowl. Johnson's takedown capped a first team All-American season as a senior with a team best 33 tackles and 5 sacks.

The number of victories (8) for the unbeaten 1912 Nittany Lions. Eugene E. "Shorty" Miller—the 5'5" quarterback for the 8-0 Nittany Lions—earned Walter Camp third team All-American honors for his part in Penn State's perfect season. Miller was inducted into the National Football Foundation College Hall of Fame in 1974.

The number of sacks (9) defensive tackle Matt Millen registered during the 1978 season. Millen was a dual threat All-American, charging after opposing quarterbacks and staying disciplined against the run with 54 total tackles. A 12-year NFL career with three different franchises followed a senior season mostly voided by injury.

The number of seasons (10) two-way lineman Glenn Ressler played for the Baltimore Colts in the National Football League. Ressler played center and middle guard in college, earning All-American honors in 1964 along with his selection as the nation's most outstanding player by Philadelphia's Maxwell Football Club. He was a member of Baltimore's 1969 Super Bowl team and the 1971 NFL championship club that defeated the Dallas Cowboys in Super Bowl V.

The total number of tackles and interceptions (11) for All-American safety Mark Robinson in the 1983 Sugar Bowl against Georgia. Robinson was credited with nine tackles and intercepted John Lastinger twice to help preserve Penn State's 27-23 victory. Robinson finished second on the team with 70 tackles and intercepted four passes during the regular season.

The number of victories (12) achieved during one season for the first time in program history during 1973. Penn State capped its first unblemished 12-game campaign with a 16-9 victory over Louisiana State in the Orange Bowl, yet again finished out of the national championship picture as fellow unbeatens Alabama and Notre Dame played for the title in the Sugar Bowl.

The single game reception record (13) achieved by Freddie Scott against Wisconsin in 1995. Scott finished his Penn State career with 93 catches for 1,520 yards and 11 touchdowns.

The number of yards covered (14) by running back Ki-Jana Carter's touchdown sprint around the left end in the final seconds of the first half in the 1994 Citrus Bowl. Offensive coordinator Fran Ganter shocked the Tennessee defense by calling Carter's number, and the running back followed a Bobby Engram block into the end zone with three seconds left. Penn State went on to dominate the second half in a 31-13 victory.

The number of consecutive defeats (15) to Penn before squeaking out a 3-3 tie at Franklin Field on October 23, 1909. Penn had dominated the series since its inception in 1890, but Penn State fought to a tie as part of a 5-0-2 season.

The number of solo tackles (16) registered by defensive end Dave Graf during the 1973 season. Graf was credited with 26 assists and one recovered fumble during the unbeaten campaign. He was part of the unit that held Pittsburgh's Tony Dorsett to 77 yards in a season ending 35-13 victory.

On November (17), 1945, freshman Wally Triplett became the first African-American player to start a Penn State game when he took the field against Michigan State. The running back did very little on the stat sheet, however, as the Nittany Lions suffered a 33-0 loss to the Spartans.

The number of rushing touchdowns (18) for Richie Anderson during the 1992 campaign. Anderson ran for 900 yards on 195 attempts for 4.6 yards per carry on the heels of a 10- touchdown season in 1991. Anderson's 28 rushing touchdowns over a two season stretch were the most since John Cappelletti's 29 rushing scores in 1972-73.

The number of rushing touchdowns (19) by Curtis Enis during the 1997 season. Enis averaged 6.0 yards per carry, totaling 1,363 yards on the ground in addition to 215 yards on 25 receptions. He broke the 100-yard rushing barrier in each of his last eight games.

The total net rushing yards (20) Penn State needed to capture its first national championship in the 1979 Sugar Bowl. Instead, in one of college football's most memorable defensive stands, Alabama stopped

Penn State's Mike Guman short of the end zone on a fourth down play inside the one yard line to preserve a 14-7 victory and the national championship. The Nittany Lions finished with 19 yards rushing, while Alabama racked up 208 yards on the ground.

The number of times (21) 1978 Lombardi Award winner Bruce Clark brought down opposing running backs and receivers behind the line of scrimmage. Clark was recognized as the nation's premier lineman/linebacker after amassing 54 tackles, 4 sacks, and 3 fumble recoveries.

The single season field goal record (22) set by Matt Bahr in 1978 and Kevin Kelly in 2006. Bahr propelled himself to the record with four field goals in a half against SMU, while Kelly attempted 34 field goals in his record tying campaign.

The program record winning streak (23) that stretched from 1968-70. The Nittany Lions finished with matching 11-0 marks in 1968 and 1969 before winning their first contest of the 1970 season.

The number of times (24) Greg Buttle brought down an opposing player during a 21-12 victory over West Virginia in 1974. The linebacker led the 1974 Nittany Lions with a single season record 165 tackles and amassed a team leading 140 takedowns the following season. He retired in 1984 after a nine year career with the New York Jets (1976-84).

The length (25) of Charles Atherton's field goal against Oberlin on November 24, 1894. Atherton, despite being ignored by historians, was the first player to kick a field goal placement from the line of scrimmage with his successful 25-yard boot on that late November afternoon.

The number of consecutive field goals (26) made by Robbie Gould as a member of the Chicago Bears from December 25, 2005–November 19, 2006. The franchise record propelled Gould to the 2006 Pro Bowl and earned him Associated Press All-Pro honors. The accolades represent a feel good story for the undrafted free agent who finished his collegiate career with 39 field goals, 22 extra points, and a 56% touchback rate on kickoffs after earning the top kicking position as a walk-on.

The length (27) of Penn State quarterback Tom Sherman's field goal in the first half of the 1967 Gator Bowl against Florida State. Sherman also threw a pair of first half touchdown passes as the Nittany Lions jumped to a 17-0 halftime lead. Florida State eventually rallied in the second half, kicking a field goal with 15 seconds remaining to force a 17-17 tie.

The number of passes (28) defended by defensive back Bhawoh Jue at Penn State from 1997-2000. Jue compiled 99 tackles and intercepted seven passes over four seasons; he also defended 16 passes as a senior—the fourth best mark in the Big Ten. The defensive back was Green Bay's Defensive Rookie of the Year in 2001, and he led San Diego with three interceptions in 2005.

The number of consecutive times (29) Penn State walked off the field against Maryland without a loss. The Nittany Lions last lost to the Terrapins, 21-17, in 1961, then ran off 24 straight victories before a 13-13 tie in 1991. Penn State regained control of the series with four more victories, including a 70-7 rout in 1993.

On December (30), 1961, Penn State topped Georgia Tech in the Gator Bowl. The Lions overcame a nine point deficit to defeat the Yellow Jackets by a score of 30-15. The announced attendance of 50,202 screaming fans witnessed Galen Hall win game MVP honors.

The number of consecutive starts (31) offensive guard Jeff Hartings made to end his collegiate career. Hartings became Penn State's 11th two-time All-American with his national recognition in 1994 and 1995.

The number of yards (32) safety Michael Zordich covered in announcing his All-American candidacy during the first minute of Penn State's 1985 season opening victory over Maryland. Zordich's interception return for a touchdown highlighted a 60 tackle campaign that earned him All-American recognition by the Football Writers and Scripps-Howard.

33 The number of tackles (33) made by defensive tackle Scott Paxson during his 2004 junior season. Paxson's breakout campaign included 8.5 tackles for losses, three sacks, and a nation best five blocked field goals.

34 The length (34) of Craig Fayak's field goal with 58 seconds left to send the 18th ranked Nittany Lions to a stunning 24-21 victory over top ranked Notre Dame on November 17, 1990. Penn State overcame a 21-7 halftime deficit.

35 The number of consecutive points (35) scored by Penn State against the Tennessee Volunteers in the 1992 Fiesta Bowl. After Tennessee quarterback Andy Kelly found a wide open Cory Fleming for a 44-yard touchdown and a 17-7 lead early in the third quarter, the Nittany Lions roared back in a big way. In less than four minutes, Penn State's defense and offense worked together to score 28 straight points, eventually leading to a 42-17 victory in Fiesta Bowl XXI.

36 The average number of return yards (36) for an Askari Adams interception in 1999. Adams tied Derek Fox and James Boyd with three interceptions, returning two of the picks for touchdowns. His long return of 59 yards boosted his season total to 108 interception return yards.

37 The number of times (37) Penn State finished in the Associated Press Top 25 final poll from 1947-2006. In addition to its two national championships, the Nittany Lions placed second on three occasions, finished in the Top 5 a remarkable 14 times, and concluded a campaign in the Top 3 four times from 1981-86.

38 The number of yards (38) linebacker Shane Conlan navigated on his second interception during the 1987 Fiesta Bowl against Miami (Fla.). Conlan led the national championship squad with 79 tackles and became Penn State's sixth two-time All-American in the process. Conlan's collegiate resume at "Linebacker U" was good enough to warrant the top overall selection by Buffalo in the 1987 NFL draft.

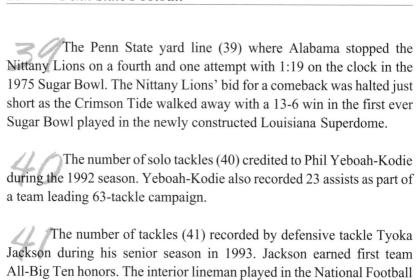

The Penn State yard line (39) where Alabama stopped the Nittany Lions on a fourth and one attempt with 1:19 on the clock in the 1975 Sugar Bowl. The Nittany Lions' bid for a comeback was halted just short as the Crimson Tide walked away with a 13-6 win in the first ever Sugar Bowl played in the newly constructed Louisiana Superdome.

The number of solo tackles (40) credited to Phil Yeboah-Kodie during the 1992 season. Yeboah-Kodie also recorded 23 assists as part of a team leading 63-tackle campaign.

The number of tackles (41) recorded by defensive tackle Tyoka Jackson during his senior season in 1993. Jackson earned first team All-Big Ten honors. The interior lineman played in the National Football League for 12 seasons with Miami, Tampa Bay, St. Louis, and Detroit.

The total points (42) scored in a 21-21 tie at Harvard on October 22, 1921. Harvard scored a late touchdown in near dark to force the tie in a game many sportswriters dubbed, "one of the greatest football games ever."

The total points (43) scored in a 27-16 victory over Army at West Point on October 8, 1960. Sam Sobczak was the first player designated as the "Hero" defensive back in the victory.

The amount of points (4.4) the Georgia Tech defense allowed per game before Penn State dropped 30 on the vaunted unit during the 1961 Gator Bowl. Penn State's victory—its third straight bowl win and its first postseason game in the South—was highlighted by Galen Hall's three touchdown passes.

The number of points (45) Penn State scored in a victory over Temple in the first night game at Beaver Stadium. The Nittany Lions won the season opener, 45-15, on September 6, 1986 behind four total touchdowns from John Shaffer.

The number of reception yards (46) tallied by Penn State's Blair Thomas during his final collegiate contest. Thomas shared game

MVP honors with BYU's Ty Detmer after racking up 232 all-purpose yards.

The number of yards (47) covered on quarterback Todd Blackledge's touchdown strike to a diving Gregg Garrity in the victory over Georgia, helping head coach Joe Paterno capture his first national championship in the 1983 Sugar Bowl. Garrity's diving grab was featured on the cover of *Sports Illustrated* and remains on the short list of top moments in program history.

The number of victories (48) Penn State recorded at Old Beaver Field. Penn State played its 49th and last game at the quaint patch of grass on November 7, 1908, defeating Bucknell, 33-6.

The number of seasons (49) between losing final records from 1938 to 1988. It all began after a 26-0 loss to Pitt on November 20, 1938 capped a 3-4-1 record. Despite the below .500 mark, Penn State set an NCAA record for fewest yards passing allowed per game (13.1 ypg).

The number of passes (50) thrown by Vinny Testaverde during the 1987 Fiesta Bowl. Over 70 million people witnessed five of those 50 attempts land in the hands of Penn State defenders on primetime television.

The number of times (51) linebacker Brandon Short brought down an opposing ball carrier behind the line of scrimmage from 1996-99. Short's ability to dictate a play on the opponent's side of the line was realized as he moved up the program's statistical charts.

The number of tackles (52) defensive end Walker Lee Ashley recorded during the 1982 national championship season. The All-American added another seven tackles to that total in the Sugar Bowl victory over Georgia. Ashley went on to a seven-year NFL career with the Minnesota Vikings (1983-88, 1990) and the Kansas City Chiefs (1989).

The number of passes (53) thrown by Bobby Hoffman during the 1955 campaign. Hoffman completed 25 of those passes for 355 yards and one touchdown. That version of the Nittany Lions won three of four down the stretch to finish with a 5-4 mark.

The year (54) in which Billy Kane needed just seven carries to scamper for 133 yards and one touchdown against Pennsylvania. Kane usually took a back seat to Lenny Moore, but he shredded the Penn defense during a 35-14 victory in 1954.

The yardage (55) placekicker Chris Bahr connected from three times during his All-American 1975 season. Bahr also recorded a 38.6 yard average on punts before taking his right foot to the National Football League with the Cincinnati Bengals (1976-79), the Oakland/Los Angeles Raiders (1980-88), and the San Diego Chargers (1989).

The most points scored in one half (56) against Illinois during the 2005 season. Penn State pounded the Illini, 63-10, as part of an 11-1 campaign that ended with a victory over Florida State in the Orange Bowl.

The seconds remaining (57) when fullback Brian Milne scored the go-ahead touchdown to lift Penn State to a 35-31 win at Illinois, clinching Penn State's first Big Ten championship after a 21-0 deficit in the first quarter. Milne's plunge capped a 15-play, 96-yard drive in the rain and wind on November 12, 1994.

The number of years (58) between Glenn Killinger's selection to the 1921 Walter Camp All-America team and the institution of the W. Glenn Killinger Football Scholarship Program at West Chester University. The quarterback was named to the All-America team after leading the Nittany Lions to two straight undefeated seasons—part of a collegiate career that included nine letters in football, basketball, and baseball. Killinger joined the faculty at West Chester (PA) State College in 1934 and served as head football and baseball coach, athletic director, and dean of men. A football scholarship was set up in his name in 1979.

The number of times (59) Fran Ganter carried the football during the 1970 season. The backup running back/fullback ran for 203 yards and three touchdowns. He played behind a trio of talented running backs (Charlie Pittman, Lydell Mitchell, and Franco Harris) during his collegiate career. Ganter served as the program's offensive coordinator from 1984-2003.

The number of years (60) between victories over Army. Quarterback Earl Hewitt returned a punt 65 yards for the only touchdown in Penn State's 6-0 victory at West Point on October 7, 1899. Penn State's next victory in the series was a 17-11 win in West Point during the 1959 campaign.

The average yards per carry (6.1) for leading rusher Curt Warner over the course of the 1981 season. Warner carried the football 171 times for 1,044 yards and 8 touchdowns during his junior campaign.

The number of tackles (62) recorded by linebacker Aaron Collins during his senior season in 1997. Collins started 36 consecutive games and made 227 career tackles as the last of five Collins brothers to play for Joe Paterno.

The single season reception record (63) set by both O.J. McDuffie in 1992 and Bobby Engram in 1995. McDuffie finished his career second on Penn State's reception list with 125 catches for 1,988 yards and 16 touchdowns. He only looks up to Engram, who caught 167 passes for 3,026 yards and 31 touchdowns.

The number of yards (64) running back Curt Warner covered on the first offensive play of the 1980 Fiesta Bowl. The touchdown sprint quickly put the Nittany Lions on top, but Ohio State scored the next 19 points to seize a double-digit lead. However, Penn State scored the game's final 24 points to claim a 31-19 victory. The contest remains Penn State's only bowl game against a Big Ten opponent.

The number of victories (65) compiled by head coach Hugo Bezdek during his 12 years at Penn State (1918-29). Bezdek guided the Nittany Lions to undefeated campaigns in 1920 and 1921 and lost just 30 games with 11 ties during his tenure. The four year All-American fullback at the University of Chicago also played second base in college and eventually coached the Pittsburgh Pirates from 1917-19. Bezdek was inducted into the National Football Foundation College Football Hall of Fame in 1954 and the Helms Foundation College Hall of Fame in 1960.

The number of times (66) John Shaffer won as a starting quarterback, encapsulating his football career from the seventh grade through his collegiate career at Penn State. Shaffer lost just once, a defeat in the 1986 Orange Bowl to Oklahoma. Shaffer completed 262 of 547 passes for 3,469 yards with 18 touchdowns and 24 interceptions as a Nittany Lion from 1983-86.

The number of tackles (67) for safety Andrew Guman during the 2004 campaign. The Academic All-American played with the same intellect on the field, recording 20 more tackles than the prior season and breaking up 7 passes.

The number of solo tackles (68) made by cornerback Anwar Phillips from 2002-05. Phillips recorded 104 total tackles with 27 pass deflections and 7 interceptions, supporting his All-Big Ten selection as a senior. He was originally signed by the New Orleans Saints shortly after the 2006 NFL draft.

The overall draft pick number (69) the New York Jets used to select linebacker Lance Mehl in the 1980 NFL draft. Mehl played with the Jets for eight seasons after an All-American collegiate career as the heart of Penn State's defense.

The negative yardage (70) defensive end Justin Kerpeikis accounted for on a team leading 18 tackles behind the line of scrimmage in 2000. Kerpeikis also recorded six sacks and compiled 76 total tackles, second on the team to James Boyd's 109. The Pittsburgh Steelers signed Kerpeikis as an undrafted free agent in 2001.

The overall draft pick number (71) the Detroit Lions used on linebacker Jim Laslavic in the 1973 NFL draft. Laslavic spent five years with the Lions and four seasons with the San Diego Chargers before ending his career in 1982 with the Green Bay Packers. The former Penn State linebacker is a member of the Western Pennsylvania Sports Hall of Fame.

The number of years (72) between Rose Bowl appearances for the Nittany Lions as they stepped onto the field in the "Granddaddy of Them All" against Oregon. A 38-20 victory over the Ducks in the 1995 Rose Bowl capped Penn State's 12-0 campaign—the fourth time Joe Paterno's Nittany Lions finished an undefeated season without a national championship.

The number of tackles (73) recorded by defensive tackle Mike McBath during the 1967 season. The run stopper made 42 solo tackles and assisted on 31 other stops while making second team All-East.

The combined number of pass deflections and tackles (74) for cornerback Derek Bochna during his 1990 freshman season. Bochna notched 56 tackles and led the team with 18 pass deflections—he also intercepted a pair of passes as a backup defensive back with one start at corner in the 1990 Blockbuster Bowl.

The number of passes (75) attempted by Milt Plum in 1956. Plum completed 40 passes for 675 yards and 6 scores. The 1956 Nittany Lions beat Ohio State and West Virginia in a 6-2-1 campaign.

The number of career receptions (76) for tight end Kyle Brady, only bested by two-time All-American Ted Kwalick among Penn State tight ends. Brady averaged 13.5 yards per catch during the 1994 season.

The number of rushing yards (77) compiled by John Chuckran in a 20-6 victory over Bucknell during the war decimated year of 1944. In Chuckran's first ever start, he needed just 15 carries and scored the game clinching touchdown with three minutes to play.

The number of rushing yards (78) running back Tony Hunt fell short of holding Penn State's all-time rushing record. Hunt was Mr. Consistency during his career in Happy Valley, using brute strength and excellent vision to dissect defenses with four and five yard runs.

The number of consecutive games (79) in which the Texas Longhorns scored a touchdown before the Nittany Lions held them out of the end zone during a 30-6 triumph in the 1972 Cotton Bowl. Penn

State's defense limited the Longhorns to 242 total yards, and running back Lydell Mitchell capped a memorable collegiate career with 146 yards rushing and one score. Head coach Joe Paterno pointed at the victory's significance after the game by saying, "It is one of the greatest victories in Penn State history."

80 The number of points (80) scored against Gettysburg at Beaver Field on October 6, 1917. Harry Robb scored six touchdowns and the Penn State defense held its in-state opponent scoreless.

81 The number of yards (81) covered on freshman Kenny Watson's kickoff return to start the second half of the 1997 Fiesta Bowl. Watson navigated 81 yards—a school bowl record—to set up Aaron Harris' five-yard touchdown run. The two-point pass from quarterback Wally Richardson to running back Curtis Enis gave Penn State a 15-12 lead in an eventual 38-15 victory over Texas.

82 The number of receptions (82) wide receiver Gregg Garrity made during his 7-year NFL career with the Pittsburgh Steelers and the Philadelphia Eagles. Garrity's career in the Keystone State began in 1983 after the Steelers selected him in the fifth-round of the draft. The wide receiver finished his career with 1,329 yards receiving and 6 touchdowns.

83 The single game rushing attempt record (83) set in a 1975 contest against rival West Virginia. The Nittany Lions used the power running game to blank the Mountaineers, 39-0.

84 The yards per carry (8.4) averaged by running back Blair Thomas during the 1986 season. Thomas spelled first team All-American D.J. Dozier and made good use of his carries for the eventual national champions. The Philadelphia native remains the only running back in school history to eclipse 1,300 yards rushing in two seasons (1987 and 1989).

85 The number of rushing yards (85) Penn State surrendered to Heisman Trophy winning tailback Marcus Allen in a 26-10 victory over Southern California in the 1982 Fiesta Bowl. Allen needed 30 carries to accumulate his season low 85 yards, while Curt Warner outshined the Trojans star with 145 yards rushing and two touchdowns.

The number of yards (86) covered on the second longest pass play in program history. Steve Joachim connected with Jim Scott for an 86-yard touchdown in a 56-3 victory over Navy in 1971. The longest pass play occurred in Pittsburgh during the 1919 season with Harold Hess finding Bob Higgins for a 92 yard score in a 20-0 victory.

The number of rushing yards (87) running back Larry Johnson blew past the 2,000-yard barrier during the 2002 campaign. Johnson became the first player in Big Ten history to surpass 2,000 rushing yards in a season, finishing with 2,087 yards and a staggering 7.7 yards per carry with 20 touchdowns. The running back took home the Maxwell, Walter Camp, and Doak Walker awards, but only placed third in the Heisman Trophy balloting.

The number of career receptions (88) for Chafie Fields. The wide receiver totaled 1,437 yards and 8 touchdowns from 1996-99. Fields is best remembered for his game-winning 79-yard touchdown catch from Kevin Thompson that beat the Miami Hurricanes, 27-23, during his senior season.

The number of interception return yards (89) for defensive back Paul Lankford during his ten year NFL career with the Miami Dolphins. Lankford played in the 1983 and 1985 Super Bowls after a solid collegiate career. The world class hurdler didn't come out for football until after the United States boycotted the 1980 Olympics.

The number of yards (90) traveled on the longest punt in Penn State history during the 1930 season. Coop French holds the record with the boot in a 19-0 loss to Iowa; however, newspaper reports printed that the punt traveled just 79 yards.

The number of victories (91) for Bob Higgins in 19 seasons as the Nittany Lions head football coach. Higgins made his Penn State name as a player, becoming one of only five players in program history to earn five letters. His coaching career included stays at West Virginia

Wesleyan and Washington University in St. Louis before he returned to Happy Valley as an assistant in 1928. Higgins became the head coach in 1930 and compiled a 91-57-11 overall record. He was inducted into the National Football Foundation College Football Hall of Fame in 1954.

The number of yards (92) covered by Mark Robinson on his punt return for a touchdown in a 49-14 victory over Rutgers in 1982. The longest punt return for a touchdown in program history came 49 years earlier when Jim Boring backed up to his own goal line and raced 100 yards for a score in a 40-6 win over Johns Hopkins.

The number of total tackles (93) for defensive tackle Ron Coder during the 1975 campaign. Coder switched from the offensive to defensive line prior to the first game, and then set out on a solid season that ended with five sacks, and led the team in passes batted down and tackles for a loss.

The team leading punt return yards (94) compiled by Dick Hoak during the 1959 season. Hoak averaged 15.3 yards per return from 1958-60 while making a name for himself as a receiver. He led the team with 14 catches for 167 yards as a junior.

The combined number of tackles and interceptions (95) for linebacker Jack Ham during the 1970 season. Ham was named to every major All-American team four years after being given Penn State's final scholarship in the 1966 recruiting class. The linebacker notched 91 tackles and four interceptions in 1970, but he went on to even bigger and better things after his stay in Happy Valley, winning four Super Bowls during a 12-year Hall of Fame career with the Pittsburgh Steelers.

The number of total tackles (96) Gary Gray registered during the 1970 season. Gray followed up that campaign with a team leading 115 tackles in 1971. Gray was always around the football, signified by level numbers of solo and assisted tackles over both campaigns.

The year (97) that Penn State improved to 6-0 when playing in the Fiesta Bowl. The Nittany Lions dismantled 1997 Big 12 champ Texas and outgained the Longhorns, 330-118, in the second half. The PSU defense held the Longhorns to minus 19 yards on the ground in the final 30 minutes.

The number of yards (98) covered on the longest interception return in school history. Wayne Berfield's interception return for a touchdown took place in 1958 against Boston University.

The number of carries (99) quarterback Rich Lucas needed to rush for a team leading 325 yards in 1959. Lucas scored six touchdowns for the 9-2 Nittany Lions, who started the season 7-0 before dropping games to a pair of nationally ranked regional rivals Syracuse and Pittsburgh.

The program reached the century mark in victories (100) with a 31-0 victory against Grove City on October 2, 1909, and then won its 200th game just over 15 years later on October 9, 1926 against Marietta.

Rip Engle, Year-by-Year Won-Loss Record

1950	Won 5, Lost 3, Tied 1
1951	Won 5, Lost 4
1952	Won 7, Lost 2, Tied 1
1953	Won 6, Lost 3
1954	Won 7, Lost 2
1955	Won 5, Lost 4
1956	Won 6, Lost 2, Tied 1
1957	Won 6, Lost 3
1958	Won 6, Lost 3, Tied 1
1959	Won 9, Lost 2
1960	Won 7, Lost 3
1961	Won 8, Lost 3
1962	Won 9, Lost 2
1963	Won 7, Lost 3
1964	Won 6, Lost 4
1965	Won 5, Lost 5

"And I want to make sure that when I do it, I do it the way
Rip Engle did it. When Rip Engle retired and gave me a shot,
he left an awful lot of meat on the bones."

— Joe Paterno at 2008 Big Ten Media Day

Chapter Two

The Man Who Created Joe Paterno

The Wing-T saved Joe Paterno from a career of lawsuits and litigation papers.

The intricate offense was Rip Engle's baby at Brown. In the base set, the halfback served as a flanker behind the end with the quarterback under center.

In 1949, that quarterback was Joseph Vincent Paterno. That season was also Engle's last along the Rhode Island shoreline. Behind the well-wishes of Engle's former college coach Dick Harlow and his Uncle Lloyd "Dad" Engle—two members of Penn State's unbeaten 1911 squad—he planned to pack his bags for the Central Pennsylvania mountains.

After turning down head jobs at Yale, Wisconsin, and Pittsburgh, Engle made one request to a Penn State athletic administration that wanted all assistant coaches to remain on staff.

He wanted to bring in Paterno, hoping to convince the 23-year-old Brooklyn boy to delay law school for a one-year stint at Engle's side.

Paterno agreed to lead Penn State's offensive transition from the well practiced Single-Wing to the more complex Wing-T. His job was to help change the offense's look before fleeing for a law degree and private practice.

He never left.

That can—in part—be credited to Engle, the only man Paterno coached under before taking his boss' job following the 1965 season. Engle took over a program prepared to take the next step up the football ladder, increasing football (grants-in-aid) scholarships to 45 and enticing such players as Dave Robinson, Lenny Moore, Milt Plum, and Richie Lucas to Happy Valley.

In Engle's 16 seasons on the job, Penn State won three Lambert Trophies as the top team in the East, claimed three bowl victories, and produced six All-Americans. Engle's teams generally finished with a flourish, winning four straight to end the 1954 campaign and rolling off five straight victories, including a Liberty Bowl rout of Oregon, to close the 1960 season.

He won 104 games with two top 11 finishes in the 1959 and 1962 Associated Press final season polls. He was inducted into the National Football Foundation College Football Hall of Fame in 1974.

When Joe Paterno won his first national championship on January 1, 1983, the moment was supposed to bring together the student and his proud teacher. Instead, Engle was battling another, more serious and debilitating opponent: Alzheimer's. He succumbed to the disease two months after Penn State's national championship, not far from the familiar Beaver Field practice grounds.

It was where Engle began his Penn State career. And it was the place where his young assistant began his Nittany Lion legacy.

Rip Engle isn't necessarily remembered for his squad's victory at second-ranked Ohio State in 1964. He isn't remembered for his team's victory over Alabama in the 1959 Liberty Bowl.

He is remembered as the man who kept a young Italian boy away from the bar exam. He is forever known as the man who created Joe Paterno.

The longest kickoff return (101) in program history occurred during a 25-0 victory over New York University in 1940. Chuck Peters took a kickoff one yard deep in the end zone and sprinted past defenders 101 yards for the score.

The triple-digit degree temperature (102) of running back John Cappelletti prior to the 1972 Sugar Bowl against Oklahoma, forcing Penn State's leading rusher out of action. The Sooners took advantage and held Penn State's makeshift running game to 46 net yards in a 14-0 victory.

The number of rushing yards (103) by Georgia Heisman Trophy winner Herschel Walker in the 1983 Sugar Bowl. Penn State running back Curt Warner bettered the Bulldog star by rushing for 117 yards on 18 attempts.

The total number of yards (104) mustered by Penn State in the 1923 Rose Bowl—the Nittany Lions' first bowl game in school history—against the University of Southern California. The 14-3 loss was attributed to only six net passing yards and a 123-yard rushing effort by Trojans running back Roy "Bullet" Baker.

The number of tackles (105) made by linebacker Jim Laslavic during the 1972 season. He played inside linebacker for a team that won ten straight after an opening loss. Laslavic played as a down rush end as a junior and made ten tackles in the first half of the 1972 Cotton Bowl against Texas.

The number of points (106) Penn State yielded to Lehigh in its all-time worst defeat on November 11, 1889. Penn State played the first half with just nine players, and the game was called with about five minutes left and the scoreboard reading 106-0. Afterward, fullback Charlie Aull was quoted as saying, "We couldn't get the son-of-a-bitch with the ball."

107 The number of receiving yards (107) for Jimmy Cefalo in a 1977 contest against Maryland. Cefalo went over the century mark one other time in his collegiate career, catching three passes for 102 yards and a touchdown in the 1975 Cotton Bowl against Baylor.

108 The number of tackles (108) defensive end Mike Hartenstine recorded during his 1974 All-American campaign. Hartenstine went on to play 13 seasons in the then NFC Central Division for the Chicago Bears (1975-86) and the Minnesota Vikings (1987).

109 The longest run from scrimmage (109) in program history. Fritz Barrett sprinted 109 yards in a 57-0 victory over Geneva in 1911. The historical significance of Barrett's run is measured far beyond one play. Barrett's run began at the one yard line on what at the time was a 110-yard football field.

110 The number of receptions (110) for Bryant Johnson during his 4-year stay in Happy Valley. Johnson accumulated 2,008 receiving yards and 10 touchdowns from 1999-2002. His best season came in 2001, when he caught 51 passes for 866 yards and 3 touchdowns.

111 The number of receiving yards (111) for wide receiver O.J. McDuffie in the 1993 Blockbuster Bowl. McDuffie supported his All-American selection with a six-catch performance that was Penn State's lone bright spot in a 24-3 loss to Stanford.

112 The number of rushing yards (112) Matt Suhey totaled in Penn State's 9-6 victory at the 1979 Liberty Bowl against Tulane. With Frank Rocco starting at quarterback for the first time that season in place of injured Dayle Tate, Suhey picked up the slack for an offense that accumulated 242 yards on the ground to minus eight yards for Tulane.

113 The number of completed passes (113) registered by quarterback Matt Knizer during the 1987 season. Knizer sat behind John Shaffer in 1985 and 1986 despite having what many believed to be a stronger, more accurate arm. He finally got his chance to start as a senior and threw for 1,478 yards and 7 touchdowns.

114 The combined number of solo tackles (114) for linebacker Lance Mehl in 1978 and 1979. Mehl registered 46 solo stops among 96 total tackles in 1978 and again led the Nittany Lions with 68 solo tackles as part of 99 total takedowns one year later. Joe Paterno said Mehl was "as good an inside linebacker" as ever played at Penn State.

115 The total number of yards (115) accumulated on Travis Forney's four field goals in the 1999 Outback Bowl against Kentucky. Forney connected from 43 yards in the first quarter, 26 yards in the second quarter, and then booted through a 21-yard chip shot and a 25-yarder in the third quarter. His school bowl record of four field goals proved to be the difference in a 26-14 victory.

116 The time remaining (1:16) when Nittany Lion quarterback Chuck Burkhart led the offense onto the field in the fourth quarter of the 1969 Orange Bowl against Kansas. Burkhart led a 50 yard touchdown march capped by his three-yard touchdown run around the left end. Coach Joe Paterno decided to attempt a game-winning, two-point conversion, but the first attempt failed. However, the Jayhawks had 12 men on the field, and Bobby Campbell scored on the next play to give the Nittany Lions a 15-14 victory to cap an 11-0 season.

117 The number of net passing yards (117) posted by quarterback Todd Blackledge during the 1980 Fiesta Bowl against Ohio State. Blackledge hit 8 of 22 passes as Penn State knocked off the Buckeyes in Tempe, Arizona.

118 The number of rushing yards (118) for running back Stephen Pitts during the 1996 Outback Bowl victory over Auburn. Pitts needed just 15 carries and scored a touchdown on a four-yard pass from Wally Richardson.

119 The number of points (119) fullback Pete Mauthe scored during the 1912 season. Mauthe not only blocked and carried the football; he also kicked it with great success. The multitalented Nittany Lion booted a 52-yard field goal and scored 11 touchdowns during his senior season. Mauthe was inducted into the National Football Foundation College Football Hall of Fame in 1957.

120 The number of interception return yards (120) David Macklin accumulated on his team best six interceptions during the 1998 season. Macklin's six picks tied him for the top spot in the Big Ten along with his 24 recorded tackles. The cornerback was taken by the Indianapolis Colts in the fourth round of the 2000 NFL draft.

121 The number of career interception return yards (121) totaled by free safety Ray Isom from 1984-86. Isom was a heavy hitter with fantastic ball instincts during his time in the defensive backfield, intercepting ten passes and laying big blows to star wide receivers. His early titanic hit on Miami Hurricanes wide receiver Michael Irvin set the tone in the 1987 Fiesta Bowl.

122 The number of rushing yards (122) for fullback Pat Botula in the 1958 season opener against Nebraska. He moved from tailback to blocking back to begin that season, and his rushing total against the Cornhuskers marked the only time he surpassed 100 yards in a game.

123 The per game, rushing yards average (129) in 1997 by AP, Football Writers, and Walter Camp All-American Curtis Enis. The Union City, Ohio native became the 12th Lion running back to earn first team All-American honors. Enis was selected by the Chicago Bears in the first round of the 1998 NFL draft.

124 The number of rushing yards (124) earned on 19 carries by running back Charlie Pittman in the 1967 Gator Bowl against Florida State. Pittman led all backs in yards gained during the 17-17 tie.

125 The number of sacks (12.5) credited to nose tackle/defensive end Pete Kugler during his 8-year NFL career. The former PSU star was a sixth-round draft pick of the San Francisco 49ers in the 1981 NFL draft. He recorded a career high 4.5 sacks in 1987.

126 The number of yards (126) opposing quarterbacks lost on defensive end Michael Haynes' 15 sacks during the 2002 season. The 15 sacks tied Larry Kubin's single season school record.

127 The number of interception return yards (127) for former Penn State safety Kim Herring throughout his 9-year NFL career with the Baltimore Ravens, the St. Louis Rams, and the Cincinnati Bengals. The safety played plenty of center field during his professional days, picking off three passes twice in a single season and finishing with eight career interceptions.

128 The total number of yards (128) of four Massimo Manca field goals against West Virginia in 1986. Manca also made a clutch 36-yard kick to down Maryland, 20-18, and keep the Nittany Lions on track for the national championship.

129 The number of receiving yards (129) totaled by wide receiver Gerald Smith during the 2002 season. Smith was the fifth option for quarterback Zack Mills, averaging 11.7 yards per catch on 11 receptions.

130 The number of tackles (130) made by linebacker Andre Collins during the 1989 season. Collins tormented opposing offenses with his ball awareness and athletic skills, totaling almost as many assists (62) as solo stops (68).

131 The number of passing first downs (131) for Penn State's high octane offense in 1994. The quartet of Kerry Collins, Ki-Jana Carter, Bobby Engram, and Kyle Brady led the prolific unit.

132 The number of team-leading kickoff return yards (132) for Owen "Doc" Dougherty in 1949. Dougherty returned 8 kicks for a 16.5 yard average. He led the team in passing during his junior season when State was still operating the Single-Wing.

133 The number of points (133) scored by the 1941 freshman team led by State's first black football player, Dave Alston. The tight end and drop-kick placekicker caught eight touchdowns, passed for four more touchdowns, and kicked six PATs.

134 The combined number of recovered fumbles and return yards (134) for linebacker Ed O'Neil during his 7-year NFL career with the Detroit Lions and the Green Bay Packers. O'Neil was Detroit's first selection in the 1974 NFL draft after a collegiate career that included first team All-American recognition as a senior. He recovered seven fumbles and returned them for 127 yards.

135 The number of sacks (13.5) for Courtney Brown in the 1999 season significantly pushed his name to the front of every All-American list. Brown also registered 55 tackles with 29 coming behind the line of scrimmage, adding to his reputation as a game-changing down lineman. For Brown's efforts, the Cleveland Browns made him the top overall selection in the 2000 NFL draft.

136 The overall draft pick number (136) the Miami Dolphins used to select defensive tackle Randy Crowder in the 1974 NFL draft. The sixth-round selection played three seasons on South Beach, and stayed in Florida for three more seasons in Tampa. Crowder was named to the All-American team as a Nittany Lion in 1973.

137 The number of passes (137) quarterback Chuck Fusina completed during Penn State's 11-0 1978 regular season. The signal caller threw for 1,859 yards and 11 touchdowns while taking home the Maxwell Award as the nation's most outstanding player.

138 The number of receiving yards (138) totaled by two-way star Don Malinak during the 1951 season. The defensive end/wide receiver caught 14 passes with two touchdowns as a sophomore.

139 The number of receiving yards (139) piled up by Bob Campbell during the 1966 campaign. Campbell was a multipurpose star with 221 yards on kick and punt returns. His best collegiate game came one year later against Navy, as he sliced through the Midshipmen for 295 all-purpose yards with 158 coming via the return game.

140 The number of rushing yards (140) accumulated by Lenny Moore in a 35-13 victory over Penn at Franklin Field on October 30, 1954. The game marked Penn State's first appearance on national television and Moore stole the show with three rushing touchdowns.

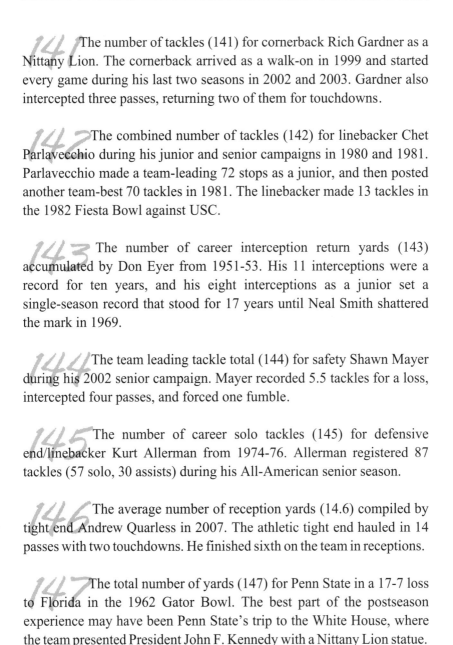

The number of tackles (141) for cornerback Rich Gardner as a Nittany Lion. The cornerback arrived as a walk-on in 1999 and started every game during his last two seasons in 2002 and 2003. Gardner also intercepted three passes, returning two of them for touchdowns.

The combined number of tackles (142) for linebacker Chet Parlavecchio during his junior and senior campaigns in 1980 and 1981. Parlavecchio made a team-leading 72 stops as a junior, and then posted another team-best 70 tackles in 1981. The linebacker made 13 tackles in the 1982 Fiesta Bowl against USC.

The number of career interception return yards (143) accumulated by Don Eyer from 1951-53. His 11 interceptions were a record for ten years, and his eight interceptions as a junior set a single-season record that stood for 17 years until Neal Smith shattered the mark in 1969.

The team leading tackle total (144) for safety Shawn Mayer during his 2002 senior campaign. Mayer recorded 5.5 tackles for a loss, intercepted four passes, and forced one fumble.

The number of career solo tackles (145) for defensive end/linebacker Kurt Allerman from 1974-76. Allerman registered 87 tackles (57 solo, 30 assists) during his All-American senior season.

The average number of reception yards (14.6) compiled by tight end Andrew Quarless in 2007. The athletic tight end hauled in 14 passes with two touchdowns. He finished sixth on the team in receptions.

The total number of yards (147) for Penn State in a 17-7 loss to Florida in the 1962 Gator Bowl. The best part of the postseason experience may have been Penn State's trip to the White House, where the team presented President John F. Kennedy with a Nittany Lion statue.

The number of rushing yards (148) by star running back Curt Warner in a 28-7 victory over Syracuse in 1982. Warner carried the football 25 times and scored twice for the Nittany Lions.

149 The number of receiving yards (149) for big-play wide receiver Bryant Johnson in a 33-7 loss to the Miami Hurricanes in 2001. Johnson caught six passes and the lone Penn State touchdown in the primetime contest at Beaver Stadium.

150 The number of games (150) played by offensive tackle Irv Pankey in his 12-year NFL career with the Los Angeles Rams and the Indianapolis Colts. Pankey was one of Penn State's best blockers during the 1970s and earned second-team All-American status at offensive guard as a senior. He also played tight end on the 1978 team and caught one pass for five yards in the 1979 Sugar Bowl.

151 The number of rushing yards (151) by tailback/fullback Joel Coles during a 21-13 victory over North Carolina State in 1980. Coles scored his first career touchdown one week later against Temple and finished the season with 406 yards on the ground. He served as the backup fullback to Jon Williams on the 1982 national championship squad.

152 The number of rushing yards (152) piled up by fullback Aaron Harris in a heartbreaking 21-20 defeat to Iowa during the 1996 season. Harris needed just 11 carries to comfortably surpass the 100-yard barrier and score one touchdown.

153 The number of receiving yards (153) racked up by running back Omar Easy during the 2000 season. Easy caught 14 passes with one touchdown reception, finishing sixth on the team in receiving yards and tied for fifth in receptions with Tony Johnson.

154 The single game bowl record for receiving yards (154) set by David Daniels in the 1990 Blockbuster Bowl against Florida State. Daniels caught a 56-yard touchdown pass from Tony Sacca and had 7 receptions in Penn State's 24-17 setback.

155 The number of interception return yards (155) safety Pete Harris traveled during his nation-best ten interceptions in 1978. Harris also recorded 28 tackles, recovered two fumbles, and broke up five passes as part of Penn State's last line of defense.

The number of games (156) coached by Rip Engle during his 16-year stint as Penn State head football coach. Engle's Nittany Lions won 104 games, came out victorious in three of four bowl games, and captured three Lambert Trophies. The head coach took home the Alonzo Stagg Award for his contributions to football in 1970.

The average yards per reception (15.7) Jack Curry had throughout his career. Curry caught 117 passes for 1,837 yards and five touchdowns from 1965-67.

The number of solo tackles (158) linebacker Jim Nelson made during his collegiate career. Nelson was a fundamentalist—chasing down and wrapping up opposing ball carriers with pinpoint technique and football IQ. Nelson also assisted on 97 tackles from 1994-97.

The number of punts (159) for Brian Masella from 1972-74. Masella and placekicker Chris Bahr formed what Joe Paterno called the "best kicking" team in Penn State history. The punter never had a punt blocked and averaged 39.3 yards per kick in 1974.

The combined number of tackles and tackles behind the line of scrimmage (160) for linebacker Dan Connor during the 2007 campaign. Connor finished seven tackles ahead of fellow linebacker Sean Lee for the team lead (145) and finished second only to Maurice Evans in the TFL (tackle for a loss) category (15).

The combined number of games started and fumbles recovered (161) for offensive guard Mike Munchak during his 12-year NFL career with the Houston Oilers. Munchak played in 159 games, made nine Pro Bowls, and earned All-Pro recognition ten times. He started 156 of those games and recovered five fumbles. Munchak, who is a member of the NFL Hall of Fame, played alongside Sean Farrell and Bill Contz on the 1982 national championship squad during his collegiate days at PSU.

The number of passes (162) completed by Michael Robinson during his senior season in 2006. Robinson threw for 2,350 yards with 17 touchdowns and 10 interceptions.

163 The number of tackles (163) for safety Calvin Lowry over 39 games, including 26 starts, as a Nittany Lion from 2002-06. Lowry built a reputation as a sure tackler and hard hitter on defense, intercepting nine passes with four recovered fumbles and two sacks. He also served as the team's primary punt return specialist, accumulating 812 yards on 86 career punt returns.

164 The total net passing yards (164) for a pair of Penn State quarterbacks in the 1986 Orange Bowl loss to Oklahoma. The Nittany Lions accumulated 267 total yards against the vaunted Sooners defense, but Oklahoma used a 71-yard touchdown pass and a 61-yard touchdown run to cement its 26-10 victory and hand Penn State its first Orange Bowl defeat.

165 The number of passing yards (165) by quarterback Elwood Petchel in Penn State's 13-13 tie against Southern Methodist in the 1948 Cotton Bowl. Petchel threw a pair of touchdown passes, including the game-tying, six-yard scoring strike to Wally Triplett in the third quarter. Ed Czekaj's extra point just missed and head coach Bob Higgins' club finished the season with a 9-0-1 record.

166 The combined number of career tackles and interceptions (166) for cornerback Brian Miller from 1993-96. Miller, who notched 154 tackles and 12 picks, led the team in interceptions during the 1994 and 1995 seasons, and despite a mid-season injury during his senior year, he racked up 115 solo tackles over his collegiate career.

167 The official playing weight in pounds (167) of defensive back Tom Bradley. Better known as "Scrap Iron" for his fearless personality on special teams, Bradley was the captain of the 1978 special teams unit known as "The Scrap Pack." The unit allowed just 87 yards on punt returns and 20 yards per kickoff return during the regular season. Bradley joined Paterno's staff as a graduate assistant in 1980 and currently heads up the defensive staff.

168 The number of career receptions (168) for tight end Ted Kwalick during his 9-year NFL career. Kwalick caught 86 passes for 1,343 yards and 10 touchdowns at Penn State. He placed fourth in the

1968 Heisman Trophy voting, leading to his first-round selection by the San Francisco 49ers in the 1969 NFL draft. The tight end also played for the Oakland Raiders and the Philadelphia Bell of the World Football League before retiring in 1977. Kwalick garnered several individual and team accolades—making three Pro Bowl appearances and collecting a Super Bowl ring from Oakland's triumph in Super Bowl XI.

The average yards per reception (16.9) Terry Smith had from 1988-91. Smith caught 108 passes for 1,825 yards and 15 touchdowns, with his best season coming in 1991.

The number of return yards (170) Gary Hayman accounted for in a 35-29 victory over North Carolina State in 1973. With the Wolfpack's focus squarely on stopping John Cappelletti, Hayman also totaled 112 receiving yards in the win.

The number of return yards (171) punt return specialist Bruce Branch accumulated over the magic number 1,000 from 1998-2001. Branch's 1,171 career punt return yards set a Penn State and Big Ten record and his 109 career punt returns placed him at the top of the program's all-time list. The return man's best season came in 1999, when he returned a single-season record 41 punts for 464 yards and two touchdowns.

The number of rushing yards (172) piled up by Bob Riggle in a 37-8 rout of West Virginia during the 1964 season. Riggle carried the football 13 times and scored twice in Penn State's convincing victory in Morgantown.

The team record for first downs (173) in a season via the ground game set by the 1971 Nittany Lions, who featured dynamic running backs Lydell Mitchell and Franco Harris.

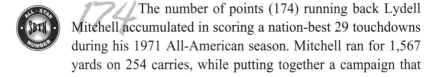

The number of points (174) running back Lydell Mitchell accumulated in scoring a nation-best 29 touchdowns during his 1971 All-American season. Mitchell ran for 1,567 yards on 254 carries, while putting together a campaign that directly led to his induction into the National Football Foundation College Football Hall of Fame in December 2004.

175 The number of receiving yards (175) gained by Bobby Engram in a 59-34 victory over Rutgers in 1995—the last time the two rivals squared off on the gridiron. Engram caught eight passes and scored three touchdowns against the Scarlet Knights.

176 The career program record for average punt return yards (17.6) set by Ron Younker from 1953-54. Younker was the main punt return specialist in 1954, racking up 193 yards on 12 returns. He drove up his average in limited duty a year earlier with four returns netting 88 yards.

177 The number of rushing yards (177) totaled by Bob "Punk" Berryman against Harvard in 1915. Berryman kept State within striking distance in a 13-0 loss, and he scored a 45 yard touchdown in a 13-3 victory over Penn during that same season.

178 The number of receiving yards (178) for two-way star Dave Robinson during the 1962 season. Robinson caught 17 passes for the 9-2 Nittany Lions, and then took his game to the NFL as a first-round draft choice of the Green Bay Packers. With the Packers, Robinson was an integral member of Coach Vince Lombardi's 1965 NFL championship squad, and the victorious Super Bowl I and II teams. He was inducted into the National Football Foundation College Hall of Fame in December 1997.

179 The number of tackles (179) recorded by defensive end Tamba Hali during his collegiate career. Hali was an offense's worst nightmare during his 2005 senior season, sacking the quarterback a Big Ten best 11 times with four coming in one game against Wisconsin. Awards soon followed and Hali was included on the first-team All-American and All-Big Ten teams. Hali was a key member of the defense that led Penn State to the 2006 Orange Bowl.

180 The official playing weight in pounds (180) of offensive guard/tackle James "Red" Bebout from 1911-13. Bebout played one of his best games in a 14-7 victory over Notre Dame in 1913. The Irish defense focused its attention on the guard, frequently yelling "Get Red, Get Red." Bebout became an officer in World War I and was killed in action on September 29, 1918 in France.

The number of rushing yards (181) pieced together by Lydell Mitchell in a 55-18 blowout of Pittsburgh in 1971. Mitchell carried the football 21 times and scored three touchdowns in Penn State's sixth straight victory over the Panthers.

The number of total yards (182) gained by the Nittany Lions in the 1979 Sugar Bowl loss to Alabama. The defensive standoff ended with Penn State's lowest yardage output in its bowl history.

The number of passes attempted (183) by Tom Shuman during the 1974 campaign. Shuman completed 97 passes with a 2:1 touchdown/interception ratio (12 touchdowns and 6 interceptions).

The number of receiving yards (184) compiled by Billy Kane throughout the 1955 season. Kane caught just nine passes good for two touchdowns, but averaged 20.4 yards per reception.

The official playing weight in pounds (185) of center Bas Gray. The Kiski Prep product entered State as a heralded recruit and lived up to the hype as the starting center on the offensive line for three seasons from 1923-25.

The program's single game bowl record for rushing yards (186) set by Blair Thomas in the 1989 Holiday Bowl against Brigham Young. Thomas carried the football 35 times and scored one touchdown against the Cougars.

The average yards per catch (18.7) for wide receiver Jimmy Cefalo during his 7-year NFL career with the Miami Dolphins. Cefalo caught 93 passes for 1,739 yards and 13 touchdowns during the regular season, and hauled in 12 passes for 297 yards and two scores in six playoff games—including two Super Bowl losses.

The number of passes (188) completed by Tom Shuman for the Nittany Lions from 1971-74. Shuman played sparingly with John Hufnagel under center in 1972, but he then threw for 1,375 and 1,355 yards in back-to-back seasons.

The number of rushing yards (189) Penn State surrendered to Missouri in the 1970 Orange Bowl—yet, the Nittany Lions defense only surrendered a field goal in a 10-3 victory, and earned their 22nd straight victory and 30th consecutive game without a defeat.

The official playing weight in pounds (190) of defensive back/linebacker Jeff Hite. The Pittsburgh, PA native joined the Penn State record books on November 4, 1974 against Maryland. He returned two interceptions for scores in the 24-17 victory. First, he intercepted · Bob Avellini and streaked down the sidelines 79 yards for a score, and then he intercepted a Maryland lateral on the kickoff and ran 21 yards for the game-winning touchdown.

The official playing weight in pounds (191) of safety and hero back Harry Hamilton. The third-team All-American contributed 100 total tackles during his senior season in 1983. His best game of the 1982 season came in the Sugar Bowl win over Georgia Tech, totaling ten tackles with one sack in a victory that gave the Nittany Lions the national championship.

The number of receiving yards (192) for tight end Isaac Smolko in 2004. Smolko hauled in 21 passes, good for third on the team, with two of Penn State's ten receiving touchdowns.

The number of passing yards (193) for Bill Smaltz in a 13-13 tie against Syracuse on November 9, 1940. Smaltz completed 12 straight passes—a record that stood until 1994.

The average number of reception yards (19.4) for wingback Lenny Krouse in the 1940 contest against Syracuse. Krouse caught eight passes, good for 155 yards and two touchdowns.

195 The number of points (195) Penn State scored during the 2004 season. The Nittany Lions struggled to score at times, averaging just 17.7 points per contest, but their defense allowed just 15.3 points per game.

196 The number of rushing yards (196) for running back Omar Easy during his 2001 senior season. Easy split carries with Larry Johnson and Eric McCoo and finished the campaign with 45 carries and one touchdown. Easy also caught nine passes for 70 yards and was selected in the fourth-round of the 2002 NFL draft by the Kansas City Chiefs, where he played sparingly for three of his four seasons.

197 The official playing weight in pounds (197) of tackle Rags Madera. The interior lineman's career was cut short by a broken thigh on a kickoff in a game against Harvard in 1921. As he was carried off the field, he yelled at his teammates to "Fight 'em State."

198 The number of rushing carries (198) by Ki-Jana Carter during the 1994 season. Carter ran for 1,539 yards and 23 touchdowns to cap a career that included 2,829 yards and 34 rushing scores.

199 The official playing weight in pounds (199) of center/linebacker Chuck Cherundolo during the mid-1930s. State struggled during the destructive years of de-emphasis in the 1930s, but Cherundolo was a bright spot in leading the team to its first victories over Syracuse in seven years (18-0) and over Bucknell in ten years (14-0) in 1936. He used to tell the defensive front, "Just take somebody out—anybody—I'll make the tackle."

200 The milestone victory (200) achieved with a 48-6 thrashing of Marietta on October 9, 1926. Ken Weston was the team captain and Hugo Bezdek was the man in charge for the 1926 Nittany Lions, who finished the season with a 5-4 mark.

John Cappelletti, Collegiate Stats

Year	Rush	YDS	AVG	TD	REC	YDS	TD	RET	YDS	TD
1971	0	0	0	0	0	0	0	43	654	0
1972	233	1,117	4.8	12	16	138	1	8	219	0
1973	286	1,522	5.3	17	6	69	0	3	16	0
Total	**519**	**2,639**	**5.1**	**29**	**22**	**207**	**1**	**54**	**889**	**0**

"No matter how sick he was he always was able to rally himself for the game. That started to be my mentality. He was doing it and so would I."

—*said John Cappelletti about his brother Joey*

Chapter Three

Joey's Heisman

*J*oe Paterno made a habit of treating positions like chess pieces—mixing and matching players based on developmental level and team need—and in 1972, the team needed John Cappelletti in the backfield after two seasons in the secondary.

Yet, despite two 1,000-yard seasons and 17 touchdowns as a senior, Cappelletti didn't take his place beside the Heisman Trophy in 1973 as a ball carrier.

He stood in front of his peers as a brother, a family man, a player driven to excellence by the painful motivation of his own blood.

"They say I've shown courage on the football field, but for me it's the time. His courage is 'round the clock."

Tick, tick, tick.

They are seconds in a game—one in which Cappelletti played better than anyone with 1,522 yards as a senior and a knack for big runs at big times.

They are also seconds in a life—one that was a struggle for Joey Cappelletti since the age of five. Leukemia made the hospital his home, and chemotherapy added nausea and headaches to his daily routine.

The disease physically wore him down in a way no football player could imagine. The game left a player battered and bruised, but the disease left a patient scarred.

And John Cappelletti knew the difference better than anybody. That's why he spent the greater part of his acceptance speech talking about "someone special," his brother Joey.

"I want him to have this trophy. It's more his than mine because he has been such an inspiration to me," said John Cappelletti.

After rushing for 100 yards 13 times, scoring 29 touchdowns, and posting 2,639 career rushing yards, John Cappelletti deserved every award imaginable. Paterno called him, "the best player I ever coached," and voters resoundingly agreed by naming him the nation's best player in 1973.

But he was a better brother. He sat by Joey's bedside as the disease took its toll. Joey died at the age of 13 after a short, but vibrant life that included a feat no one his age had ever accomplished.

At the age of 11, he accepted the Heisman Trophy.

201 The number of all-purpose yards (201) racked up by running back Leroy Thompson in the 1988 Citrus Bowl against Clemson. Thompson showcased his speed and vision with 127 kickoff return yards and added 19 yards receiving and 55 yards rushing as part of a dual rushing attack in place of injured star tailback Blair Thomas. Gary Brown received the bulk of the carries with 13 attempts for 51 yards in the Nittany Lions' first bowl appearance in Orlando (a 35-10 loss to Clemson).

202 The number of yards (202) gained by Tulane in the 1979 Liberty Bowl. Penn State outgained the Green Wave by 135 yards in the battle of placekickers. The final boot came with 18 seconds remaining, when PSU prevailed 9-6 after a 20-yard, game-winner off the foot of Herb Menhardt.

The overall selection (203) the Pittsburgh Steelers used to take safety Darren Perry in the eighth round of the 1992 NFL draft. Perry played seven of his nine NFL seasons with the Steelers before getting into coaching. The 1991 All-American picked off six passes during his senior season, including back-to-back interception returns for touchdowns against Boston College and Temple.

The number of rushing yards (204) posted by John Cappelletti against Ohio University on 25 touches during the 1973 season. Cappelletti rushed for over 200 yards three times during his career. His highest tally came against North Carolina State with 220 yards and three touchdowns in 1973.

The number of passes (205) attempted by Jack White during the 1965 campaign. White completed 98 passes for 1,275 yards and six touchdowns. White led the Nittany Lions to a 5-5 record capped by a 19-7 victory over Maryland.

The number of rushing yards (206) compiled by true freshman Eric McCoo in a 51-28 rout of Michigan State during the 1998 season. McCoo eclipsed the 200-yard mark and set the single game school rushing record by a freshman in the victory over the Spartans at Beaver Stadium.

The single season interception return yards record (207) set by cornerback Alan Zemaitis in 2003. Zemaitis' interception return yards also set a single season Big Ten record.

The number of completions (208) for Anthony Morelli during the 2006 season. Morelli completed 208 of 386 passes for 2,424 yards with 11 touchdowns and 8 interceptions.

The number of net rushing yards (209) gained by Penn State during the 1994 Citrus Bowl against the #6 Tennessee Volunteers. PSU beat the Vols in front of a Citrus Bowl record 72,456 fans. The win gave the Lions a 10-2 record and a Top Ten finish in the polls.

The number of passing yards (210) tallied by senior Anthony Morelli on 22 of 35 pass attempts against Purdue on November 3, 2007. PSU won the contest, 26-19, as Morelli became the first quarterback in Penn State history to throw for over 2,000 yards in back-to-back seasons.

The average number of passing yards per game (211) by the PSU offense during the 2007 regular season. The Lions ended the season with a 9-4 mark and an Outback Bowl victory over Tennessee.

The total number of tackles (212) for free safety Kim Herring during his college career. The three-year starter not only crept up into the box on obvious running downs, but his ball instincts led to 13 career interceptions with seven coming during his senior season.

The total number of tackles (213) defensive tackle Jimmy Kennedy recorded during his four-year stay in Happy Valley. Kennedy was sometimes overshadowed by pass rusher Michael Haynes and tackle machine Shawn Mayer, but he put up consistent numbers with his top season, an 87-tackle effort in 2002. Kennedy finished right behind Haynes with 16 tackles for a loss and 5.5 sacks as a senior.

The single season program record for average punt return yards (21.4) set by Don Jonas in 1960. Jonas only returned seven punts but tallied 150 yards and one touchdown. During his collegiate career from 1958-61, Jonas returned 17 punts for 271 yards and two scores.

The number of passing yards (215) Matt Knizner compiled through the air in a 35-21 victory over Rutgers in 1987. Knizner had one other 200-yard passing game and finished the season with 1,478 yards passing and seven touchdowns.

The single game receiving yardage record (216) amassed by Deon Butler in a 2006 victory over Northwestern. Butler also holds the single game record for receiving yardage by a freshman with 125 yards against Wisconsin in 2005.

The number of kick return yards (217) for Rich Mauti during the 1976 season. The tailback/wide receiver averaged 16.7 yards per kick return and also returned 17 punts for 208 yards.

The total number of rushing yards (218) for Penn State tailbacks Steve Geise (111) and Bob Torrey (107) in the 1977 Fiesta Bowl. Torrey needed just seven carries to slice through the Arizona Wildcats defense while Geise served as the workhouse with 26 rushing attempts. In total, the Nittany Lions outrushed the Wildcats, 268-90, in a 42-30 victory.

The Penn State record for number of first half passing yards (219) set by Mike McQueary against Wisconsin in 1997. McQueary finished the season with 2,211 yards on 146 of 255 passing, with 17 touchdowns and 9 interceptions.

The official playing weight in pounds (220) for fullback Franco Harris during the 1971 season. Harris was selected as the #13 overall pick in the 1972 NFL draft by the Pittsburgh Steelers.

The number of rushing yards (221) Penn State's offense compiled against Ohio State in 1964. Offensive tackle Joe Bellas helped pave the way during that game and throughout the season, garnering more playing time than any other player.

The number of career rushing attempts (222) by Penn State's Bob Torrey from 1976-78. Torrey finished his Penn State career with 1,095 rushing yards and 3 touchdowns.

The official playing weight in pounds (223) of linebacker/defensive end Terry Killens. The sack specialist found his true calling as an undersized rush end during the 1995 season with 13 sacks, counting two in the 1996 Outback Bowl victory over Auburn.

The combined number of receptions, receiving yards, and touchdowns (224) for wide receiver O.J. McDuffie in a 1992 contest against Boston College. McDuffie tallied 11 receptions, 212 receiving yards, and one touchdown—he also racked up 43 yards on the ground and 24 yards in kick returns against the Eagles.

The number of points (22.5) the Nittany Lions averaged per contest during the 2001 season. Penn State did most of its damage just after halftime, outscoring its opponents 81-55 in the third quarter.

The number of tackles (226) for linebacker Rogers Alexander from 1982-85. Alexander was steady, if not flashy, as the defensive leader of the 1985 team that finished unbeaten and played Oklahoma for the national title at the 1986 Orange Bowl. He led the team in tackles with 102 on 54 solos with 48 assists.

The number of rushing yards (227) gained by running back Ki-Jana Carter in the 1994 regular season finale against Michigan State. He reached the end zone five times against the Spartans, totaling his 23 touchdowns during a season highlighted by an 83-yard touchdown sprint on Penn State's first play from scrimmage in the Rose Bowl, and an individual portfolio that left him second in the Heisman Trophy race behind Colorado running back Rashaan Salaam.

The official playing weight in pounds (228) of offensive lineman Tom Jackson, who shuffled between guard and tackle from 1967-69. He served as the offensive captain, along with defensive captains Mike Reid and Steve Smear, during the 1969 campaign.

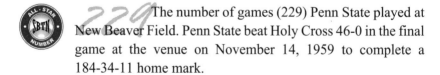

The number of games (229) Penn State played at New Beaver Field. Penn State beat Holy Cross 46-0 in the final game at the venue on November 14, 1959 to complete a 184-34-11 home mark.

The number of sacks (23.0) Tim Johnson registered with the Washington Redskins (20.5) and the Cincinnati Bengals (2.5). The pass rusher also registered 8.5 sacks during three seasons with the Pittsburgh Steelers. Johnson was selected in the sixth round of the 1987 NFL draft by the Steelers after a standout senior campaign at Penn State that concluded with All-American honors. He also won a Super Bowl ring with the Redskins in Super Bowl XXVI.

The number of points (231) scored by the Nittany Lions during the 1988 season. The defense held opponents to just 201 points, but the Nittany Lions still finished with a disappointing 5-6 mark.

The number of penalty yards per game (23.2) registered against Penn State in the 2003 season. The Nittany Lions were a disciplined football team compared to their opponents, which averaged 51 yards in penalties per contest.

The official playing weight in pounds (233) of linebacker/defensive end Joe Lally. The rush end was a steady presence on a star-studded defensive line that featured Bruce Clark, Matt Millen, and Larry Kubin. He recovered a fumble at the 19-yard line during the fourth quarter of the 1979 Sugar Bowl, setting up the famous fourth and inches goal line stand by Alabama.

The official playing weight in pounds (234) of linebacker Keith Goganious. The Virginia Beach, VA native blossomed as an upperclassman, registering 55 tackles as the starter at inside linebacker during his senior season. Goganious averaged eight tackles per game as a junior in 1990 and led the team in tackles four times that season, including the 1991 Blockbuster Bowl against Florida State.

The total number of sacks (23.5) by linebacker LaVar Arrington over seven NFL seasons with the Washington Redskins and the New York Giants. The three-time Pro Bowl representative's best statistical season came in 2001 with the Redskins, when he sacked the quarterback 11 times with nearly 100 tackles. Arrington won the 1999 Chuck Bednarik and Dick Butkus awards as a Nittany Lion and was selected by Washington with the second overall pick in the 2000 NFL draft.

The number of receiving yards (236) compiled by Ethan Kilmer on 15 catches during the 2005 season. Kilmer walked on to the team after attending Shippensburg (Pennsylvania) University for two years and started out on defense at safety. He starred on special teams in 2004 and then moved to the opposite side of the football at wide receiver one season later. Kilmer closed his career in the 2006 Orange Bowl with a 6-catch, 79-yard performance that included a 24-yard touchdown.

237 The number of career tackles (237) defensive tackle Jim Heller recorded from 1970-72. He totaled 133 solo tackles and 104 assists, yet never led the team in any one season. Joe Paterno said of Heller, "He's an extremely dedicated football player and leader who is one of the finest defensive tackles in the East."

238 The official playing weight in pounds (238) of linebacker Don Graham. A part of the "sack gang" on the 1985 and 1986 squads, Graham led the team in sacks in 1985 (seven) and 1986 (nine) before taking his knack for sacks to the NFL as the Atlanta Falcons fourth-round draft choice in the 1987 NFL draft.

239 The number of rushing yards (239) for Bobby Campbell during a 30-12 victory over Syracuse on December 7, 1968. Campbell needed just 24 carries to amass the large rushing game, which included an 87-yard touchdown sprint.

240 The official playing weight in pounds (240) of center Warren Koegel. The offensive lineman snapped the football for Joe Paterno's back-to-back unbeaten squads of 1968 and 1969. Koegel was the Oakland Raiders' third choice in the 1971 NFL draft. He played one year with the Raiders and another with the St. Louis Cardinals and the New York Jets.

241 The number of career tackles (241) for strong safety/linebacker Brian Chizmar from 1986-89. Chizmar recorded 161 solo tackles and 80 assists while lining up just behind teammate and star linebacker Andre Collins. He totaled 110 of those tackles during his senior campaign.

242 The number of completions (242) for Rashard Casey from 1997-2000. Casey finally got his chance to shine in 2000 after waiting behind Mike McQueary and Kevin Thompson, throwing for 2,001 yards and 14 touchdowns. Five of those 14 scoring passes came in a 67-7 rout of Louisiana Tech, tying the single game touchdown pass record first set by Tony Sacca in a 34-22 victory over Georgia Tech in 1991.

The number of receptions (243) by tight end Troy Drayton during his 8-year NFL career with the Los Angeles/St. Louis Rams, Miami Dolphins, and Kansas City Chiefs. Drayton racked up 2,645 receiving yards with 24 touchdowns after a steady collegiate career as a Nittany Lion from 1989-92.

The official playing weight in pounds (244) of center Chuck Correal, who manned the middle of Penn State's offensive line for the great 1978 squad that lost to Alabama in the national championship game at the 1979 Sugar Bowl. Correal was an eighth-round pick of the Philadelphia Eagles in the 1979 NFL draft, but played in the NFL for the Atlanta Falcons (1979-80) and the Cleveland Browns (1981).

The number of sacks (24.5) Tyoka Jackson registered as a member of the Nittany Lions defense. Jackson rose out of his stance and mauled opposing linemen on his way to the quarterback with regularity, leading the team in sacks during his sophomore (9.5) and senior (8) campaigns. Jackson's total, however, still puts him well behind Courtney Brown's record 33 sacks.

The official playing weight in pounds (246) of defensive end/tight end Kirk Bowman during his four year stay in Happy Valley from 1980-83. Bowman is best known as a pass catcher in a 1982 regular season victory over Nebraska. The tight end caught a low pass from Todd Blackledge in the back of the end zone, and then hauled in the game-winning 14-yard touchdown pass in a 27-24 victory. He didn't record a catch for the remainder of the season.

The average interception percentage (2.47) for quarterback Pete Liske in 1962. His career interception percentage of 2.82 was the record before John Sacca bested the mark in 1993.

The number of passing yards (248) Penn State surrendered through the air to Florida State quarterback Casey Weldon during the 1990 Blockbuster Bowl. The total was the second highest allowed by the

Nittany Lions all season. Penn State's starting quarterback Tony Sacca was replaced by senior Tom Bill late in the fourth quarter.

The number of rushing carries (249) for Roger Kochman during the 1961 and 1962 seasons. Penn State finished 8-3 and 9-2 under the leadership of Rip Engle.

The number of games (250) won by Joe Paterno following a 31-0 victory on the road at Iowa on September 18, 1993. The defense set up three scores and registered nine sacks in the Big Ten contest.

The number of times (251) Penn State made an appearance on television from Joe Paterno's first season in 1966 through the 2007 Outback Bowl. Penn State compiled a 159-91-1 record during that time, including a 22-10-1 record in bowl games.

The official playing weight in pounds (252) of offensive tackle Bill Contz. The 6' 6" blocker began his collegiate career on the defensive side of the football before moving to offense as a sophomore.

The Lions single game bowl record for passing yards (253) set by Michael Robinson in the 2006 Orange Bowl against Florida State. Robinson completed 21 of 39 passes with one touchdown and one interception in the 26-23 triple overtime victory over the Seminoles.

The number of sack yards (254) amassed by Penn State's defense during the 2002 season. Michael Haynes and Jimmy Kennedy led a defensive unit that registered 35 sacks. On the other side of the football, the Nittany Lions offensive line yielded just 18 sacks.

The total number of sacks (25.5) linebacker Andre Collins delivered to opposing quarterbacks during his NFL career with the Washington Redskins, the Cincinnati Bengals, and the Chicago Bears. Collins was a member of Washington's Super Bowl XXVI championship team and recorded a career best 6.0 sacks in both 1990 and 1993. The All-American at Penn State was a Butkus Award finalist in 1989.

The number of tackles (256) Trey Bauer totaled f 1984-87. Bauer recorded a career best 94 tackles in 1985, including 2 takedowns in a 17-10 victory over Rutgers.

The total number of minutes (257) in Penn State's wild 50-39 victory over Brigham Young in the 1989 Holiday Bowl. The 4-hour, 17-minute affair included 64 second half points, 1,115 total yards, 61 first downs, and just three punts.

The official playing weight in pounds (258) of offensive guard John Nessel. Nessel played on the offensive line in 1973 and 1974, helping John Cappelletti win the Heisman Trophy in 1973. He became the first offensive lineman of the Joe Paterno era to earn All-American recognition in 1974.

The number of receiving yards (259) racked up by tight end John Gilmore during the 1999 season. Gilmore and Tony Stewart provided a solid one-two punch around the goal line and in the middle of the field. Running back Eric McCoo and Gilmore each caught 22 passes that season, just behind Eddie Drummond and Chafie Fields on the statistical charts.

The number of fans over 60,000 (260) that witnessed Penn State's 42-14 rout of Pitt on November 28, 1981 — killing the Panthers' national championship aspirations. Roger Jackson and Mark Robinson helped the Penn State cause by intercepting heralded Pitt quarterback Dan Marino.

The number of rushing yards (261) Mike Cerimele grinded out on the ground during the 1998 season. Cerimele was used as a goal line halfback and blocking back for Eric McCoo.

The number of yards (262) Todd Blackledge threw for in a 39-31 victory over Maryland on September 11, 1982. Blackledge tossed four touchdown passes to just two for Terrapins signal caller Boomer Esiason in Penn State's 100th victory at Beaver Stadium.

)verall draft pick number (263) used by the
Penn State's Frank Giannetti in the 1991 NFL
d was selected as the 13th pick of the tenth round.
took his teammate Sean Love with the next

The number of carries (264) it took running back Blair
Thomas to accumulate 1,341 yards during his 1989 senior campaign, a
remarkable season that included eight 100-yard games with major
reconstructive knee surgery in the rearview mirror. Thomas totaled 3,301
rushing yards and 4,512 all-purpose yards during his distinguished
career.

The number of points (26.5) Penn State averaged per
contest during the 1998 season. The Nittany Lions outscored their
opponents by nearly 11 points per game in defensive coordinator Jerry
Sandusky's second to last season on staff.

The official playing weight in pounds (266) of offensive
guard Sean Farrell. The two-time, first-team All-American earned the
praise of head coach Joe Paterno as the first three-year starter at offensive
guard in 20 years. At the end of his career, Paterno theorized, "If there's a
better guard in the country (than Farrell), he's Superman."

The overall draft pick number (267) used by the Cincinnati
Bengals on Penn State's Tom DePaso in the 1978 NFL draft. The
linebacker was selected as the 17th pick of the tenth round.

The number of yards (268) Penn State's defense
surrendered to West Virginia in a 27-0 victory on Homecoming in 1985.
John Shaffer tossed two touchdown passes and the defense forced two
fumbles, registered four sacks, and intercepted three passes in the
program's 600th victory.

The average number of kick return yards (26.9) for Gary
Harman during his collegiate career. Harman led both the 1972 and 1973
squads in kickoff and punt returns, and stood atop the country with a
19.2-yard punt return average in 1973. His lone career kickoff return for a

touchdown came in a 1973 game against Maryland, when he sprinted 93 yards for the score.

The official playing weight in pounds (270) of defensive end/defensive tackle Lou Benfatti from 1990-93. Benfatti remains one of the few players in the Paterno era to start every game from his freshman season through senior year (49 total). He garnered first-team All-American recognition as a senior and second team consideration one year earlier.

The number of rushing attempts (271) by Larry Johnson during his 2002 campaign. The blue and white faithful witnessed Johnson set the single-season rushing record, breaking Lydell Mitchell's 30-year-old rushing record by over 500 yards.

The number of sack yards (272) totaled by the 2006 Nittany Lions defense. Tamba Hali and Jay Alford led a defense that registered 41 sacks. On the flip side of the football, Penn State's offensive line surrendered just 19 sacks.

The number of tackles (273) linebacker Brandon Short made during his collegiate career. Short was a tackling machine, finishing with ten or more stops six times during the 1999 season.

The number of tackles (274) credited to John Skorupan from 1970-72. While Ed O'Neil led the team with 126 tackles in 1972, Skorupan earned All-American honors with a 106-tackle season that included 15 takedowns against Navy.

The number of rushing yards (275) for Booker Moore during his 1983 season with the Buffalo Bills. Moore also caught 34 passes for 199 yards and one of his two career touchdowns for the Bills. The undrafted running back struck a solid balance of rushing and receiving throughout his four-year career in Buffalo, rushing for 420 yards and hauling in 75 passes for 423 yards. Moore never led the Nittany Lions in rushing from 1977-80.

The total number of points (276) scored by placekicker Brett Conway from 1993-96. His right leg won games for six different NFL teams from 1997-2003, including two tours of duty with the Washington Redskins.

The team record for first downs in a season (277) set by the 2002 Nittany Lions, who finished off a 9-4 campaign with a hard fought 13-9 loss to Auburn in the 2003 Capital One Bowl. Penn State lost each of its four games by a touchdown or less.

The career-best passing yards (278) compiled by Matt Senneca in a 2001 victory over Indiana. Senneca completed 17 of 23 passes with one touchdown and one interception in the 28-14 win. The veteran quarterback was eventually replaced by freshman Zack Mills after throwing for 755 yards, three scores, and five interceptions.

The Penn State record for number of rushing yards (279) gained in the first half by Larry Johnson against Michigan State in 2002. Johnson ran all over the Spartans on 19 carries in the first 30 minutes.

The official playing weight in pounds (280) of offensive tackle Chris "Bucky" Conlin. The 1986 first-team All-American opened holes for star halfback D.J. Dozier and the fullback duo of Tim Manoa and Steve Smith. The Miami Dolphins' fifth-round selection in the 1987 NFL draft played two years in south Florida and three more in Indianapolis before leaving pro football behind.

The official playing weight in pounds (281) for tackle Bill Dugan during the 1980 season. The lineman was selected to the first-team All-America squad and was then drafted by the Seattle Seahawks as the second pick in the third round of the 1981 NFL draft.

The career scoring record (282) set by Craig Fayak. The placekicker made 50 field goals and added 132 extra points from 1990-93.

The total yard differential (283) between the Nittany Lions and Miami Hurricanes in the 1987 Fiesta Bowl. Miami racked up 445 yards to just 162 for Penn State, but the Nittany Lion defense caused seven turnovers to capture their second national championship.

284   The number of receiving yards (284) piled up on 25 catches by tight end John Gilmore during his 2001 co-captain season. Gilmore, a four-year letter winner, was picked by the New Orleans Saints in the sixth round of the 2002 NFL draft before signing with the Chicago Bears later that year. Gilmore left Penn State with a degree in Recreation and Parks Management.

285   The number of points (285) scored by the undefeated 1912 squad. James Lester Mauthe was selected by Walter Camp as a third-team All-American, as the Nittany Lions outscored their opponents 285-6.

286   The number of carries (286) running back John Cappelletti needed to amass 1,522 yards during his 1973 Heisman Trophy winning season. Cappelletti rushed for 17 touchdowns and posted a then-NCAA record of three consecutive 200-yard plus rushing performances, including a 220-yard effort against North Carolina State.

287   The number of sack yards (287) compiled by the Penn State defense during the 1998 campaign. Courtney Brown led the way with 11 sacks and Brad Scioli added 10 for a team best 89 yards in losses. The Nittany Lions not only got after opposing quarterbacks with 47 sacks — they protected their quarterbacks by allowing just 26 sacks on the season.

288   The list price in January 2008 on Amazon.com ($2.88) for a used copy of the 1971 hardcover edition of *Joe Paterno: Football My Way* by Mervin Hyman and Gordon White.

289   The number of rushing yards (289) collected by Penn State during its November 9, 2002 meeting with Virginia. In front of 108,698 screaming fans, Larry Johnson gained 188 yards on 31 carries. The Nittany Lions defense held the Cavaliers to 30 yards on the ground in a 35-14 victory.

The number of receiving yards (290) racked up by Bobby Engram during his 2006 season with the Seattle Seahawks. The 1996 second-round draft choice was Seattle's leading receiver in 2005, but had a major drop off in 2006 after being diagnosed with Graves disease, which caused him to have an accelerated heart rate, weight loss, and debilitating fatigue. He returned to form through hard work and posted over 1,000 yards in 2007.

The number of receiving yards (291) accumulated by three-sport athlete Jesse Arnelle during the 1953 season. Arnelle was best known as a first-team All-American hoops star, but he lined up out wide and caught 33 passes with two touchdowns during his sophomore campaign.

The number of pass attempts (292) by PSU quarterbacks Tony Sacca during the 1991 season and Todd Blackledge during his 1982 campaign. Both passers began their careers as game managers and evolved into experienced game changers during their junior and senior seasons.

The total number of net yards gained (293) by the University of Southern California during the 1923 Rose Bowl against the Nittany Lions. Penn State traveled by train from State College to Pasadena with stops in Chicago and at the Grand Canyon—but suffered a 14-3 loss to USC in the first postseason game in school history.

The previous NFL record for most return yards in a single game (294) set by former Penn State great Wally Triplett during a 1950 NFL game between Triplett's Detroit Lions and the Green Bay Packers. While at PSU, Triplett became the first African American to play in a Cotton Bowl, and upon graduation he became the first African American to be both formally drafted and play in the NFL.

The number of receiving yards (295) compiled by wide receiver Mike Alexander with the Los Angeles Raiders in 1989. The eighth-round draft choice out of PSU caught 15 passes and one NFL touchdown over 16 games.

The career record for kickoff return average (29.6) held by Larry Joe, who returned 16 kickoffs for 473 yards with one touchdown from 1946-48. Joe's best season was in 1947 with nine kickoff returns totaling 293 yards for a 32.6 yard average.

The number of points (297) scored by the Nittany Lions during the 1990 season while holding their opponents to just 179 points. PSU finished the year with a 9-3 record and victories over five teams with winning records, including victories over marquee programs Notre Dame and Alabama.

The career high passing yards (298) posted by quarterback Anthony Morelli at Illinois on September 29, 2007. Morelli completed 21 of 38 passes and piled up large passing numbers; however, three interceptions inside the Illini 30-yard line allowed the host team to escape with a 27-20 victory.

The official playing weight in pounds (299) of offensive tackle Andre Johnson. The three-year starter was a key member of the 1995 Rose Bowl championship team and an offensive line that yielded just three sacks all season.

The career victory mark (300) topped by both Joe Paterno and Alabama head coach Paul "Bear" Bryant. The two tradition-rich programs sold out the Louisiana Superdome in the first of four meetings between the two legends in the 1975 Sugar Bowl.

2002 Heisman Voting Results

Player	School	1st	2nd	3rd	Total
Carson Palmer	Southern Cal	242	224	154	1,328
Brad Banks	Iowa	199	173	152	1,095
Larry Johnson	*Penn State*	*108*	*130*	*142*	*726*
Willis McGahee	Miami	101	118	121	660
Ken Dorsey	Miami	122	89	99	643
Byron Leftwich	Marshall	22	26	34	152
Jason Gesser	Washington State	5	22	15	74
Chris Brown	Colorado	5	11	11	48
Kliff Kingsbury	Texas Tech	6	2	11	33
Quentin Griffin	Oklahoma	1	8	9	28

"I was just running, I was running in a straight line and I couldn't see too much and I didn't really realize until after I sat down that it happened."

—Larry Johnson on his run that broke the 2,000-yard barrier in 2002

Chapter Four

Patience is a Virtue for a Family of Nittany Lions

*I*t had to be difficult. Dressing for a game he wouldn't play. Looking from the sidelines at a field he wouldn't see.

After running from State College to Altoona and back again—a trip that racked up 2,159 yards and 29 touchdowns during his senior season for the Little Lions—Larry Johnson had to figure his ascension to greatness would be rapid, his transition to the Penn State backfield seamless.

Johnson's raw talent would need no adaptation. He was joining his father and defensive line coach Larry, Sr., and one year later his brother and wide receiver Tony Johnson, a few blocks from his front doorstep in Happy Valley.

It appeared to be a match made in heaven—at any other football program, under any other head football coach.

Not Joe Paterno. Not in a program hierarchy rooted in equal parts talent and longevity. In Paterno's eyes, if a player worked hard and paid his dues, he was afforded an ironclad chance at playing time.

What a player did with that opportunity was up to him. Unfortunately for Johnson, his path to the backfield (and a list of Penn State rushing records) was blocked by Eric McCoo—a Red Bank, NJ product without the hometown buzz or the NFL size.

Standing roughly three inches shorter and some 20 pounds lighter than Johnson, McCoo played much too well for many supporters to notice Johnson's highlights on special teams and in mop-up duty.

Johnson finally saw the light at the end of a dark, bleak tunnel during McCoo's senior season. Whether he was too eager, too immature, or too bitter from two years wasted on the middle rung of the depth chart, a perceived rift developed between coach and player during his junior season.

He led the team in rushing (337 yards and 2 touchdowns) despite less attempts than McCoo and quarterback Zack Mills, a signal caller with nimble footwork but little in the speed department.

Frustration could have boiled over to contempt. Yet, the oldest of three Penn State athletes in the family (sister Teresa played third base on the softball team) listened to his father's guidance.

A man who counseled his son and worked alongside the coach at the front of the difficulty preached patience and work ethic.

The message, spoken through the body language of a coach and father, was simple.

The chance will come. Be ready.

Johnson did just that, and by the time his senior season came to an end, area newspapers and Nittany Lion play-by-play announcer Steve Jones were rejoicing, "2K for LJ."

The climb to the top included smashed records and numerous honors. Johnson ran past Penn State's lone Heisman Trophy winner John Cappelletti. He sprinted past Lydell Mitchell and Charlie Pittman. He eventually surpassed Curt Warner, breaking many of their records and even shattering some of his own.

Johnson had twice set the single game rushing record heading into a November 16, 2002 meeting at Indiana. He ran over Northwestern's defense for 257 yards, and then totaled 279 yards against Illinois.

Both were prodigious piles of yards—each almost matching his entire junior season rushing output.

Then came the late fall Saturday at Memorial Stadium. He scored on runs of 69, 43, 1, and 41 yards against Indiana. Those carries totaled 154 of his new single game record 327 yards—the game of a lifetime that fell just 50 yards shy of Anthony Thompson's conference record for rushing yards in a game.

"I never thought I'd go out and do what I did today," stated an almost apologetic Johnson, who also broke Mitchell's single season rushing mark on that Saturday.

He almost sounded sorry. Not for something he did or said to others, but for the creeping doubts that entered his mind following three seasons in obscurity.

That was finally in the past. He had rewritten history on his way to Heisman Trophy consideration. He had found a deeper appreciation for the life lessons of his head coach. And he had discovered that two clichés were in fact true.

Patience is a virtue. And father does know best.

The third highest bowl game rushing total (301) achieved by the Nittany Lions in the 1960 Liberty Bowl. Dick Hoak led the way with 61 yards rushing and two touchdowns as Penn State pounded Oregon, 41-12.

The number of all-purpose yards (302) Harry Wilson compiled in a 21-3 victory over the Naval Academy in 1923. Wilson ran for 115 yards and racked up 187 return yards in the home game against Navy. Wilson starred in all phases of the game later that season at Pennsylvania with 278 all-purpose yards in a 21-0 victory.

The number of receiving yards (303) gained by Harold Powell during the 1957 season. Powell hauled in 32 passes and scored three touchdowns—but he caught nine of those passes in a 17-14 victory over UCLA in the season opener.

The official playing weight in pounds (304) of defensive tackle Brandon Noble during his time with the Dallas Cowboys. Noble bounced around between San Francisco's practice squad and NFL Europe before catching on with the Cowboys in 1999. The former Nittany Lion was signed by the Redskins but missed the entire 2003 campaign after a left knee injury. Since then, Noble has been dealing with methicillin-resistant Staphylococcus aureus (MRSA), a sometimes debilitating staph infection.

The number of points (305) scored by Kevin Kelly from 2005-07. Kelly is Penn State's all-time leading scorer. He sits 143 points above fellow placekicker Travis Forney.

The combined number of receiving yards (306) for safety valves R.J. Luke (207) and Mick Blosser (99) during the 2001 season. Both tight end/blocking ends caught 12 passes, with Luke exploiting the defense for 17.2 yards per catch. Quarterbacks Zack Mills and Matt Senneca only found four receivers more times than this duo during the regular season.

The number of receptions (307) for Hall of Fame running back Franco Harris during his illustrious 13-year NFL career. Harris played 12 of his 13 NFL seasons with the Pittsburgh Steelers, making nine Pro Bowls and eclipsing 1,000 yards eight times. The running back ran for 12,120 yards and 91 touchdowns and totaled 2,287 receiving yards with nine more scores. His 14,622 yards from scrimmage ranked as the third highest total in pro football history at the time of his retirement. Harris rushed for 2,002 yards and 24 touchdowns for the Nittany Lions from 1969-71.

The number of receiving yards (308) accumulated by running back Tim Manoa during his brief four-year NFL career with the Cleveland Browns and the Indianapolis Colts. Manoa's best season came as the Browns starting fullback in 1989, when he posted 289 rushing yards with three touchdowns and 241 receiving yards with two more scores. Manoa served as D.J. Dozier's lead blocker and carried the football eight times for 36 yards in the 1987 Fiesta Bowl.

The number of passes (309) Rashard Casey threw during the 2000 season. Casey also finished third on the team in rushing with 315 yards and tied Eric McCoo with a team-best five rushing touchdowns.

The number of return yards (310) compiled by running back Lenny Moore during the 1955 season. Moore ran for 697 yards and added another 37 yards receiving for a team best 1,044 all-purpose yards.

The combined number of rushing and receiving yards (311) accumulated by running back Wally Triplett during his rookie season with the Detroit Lions in 1949. Triplett tallied 221 yards on the ground and 90 more through the air; he also scored his only career touchdown during the campaign. The running back was a three year letterman at Penn State.

The combined number of interception return and kickoff return yards (312) for defensive back Mark Robinson during his NFL career from 1984-91. Robinson scampered 215 yards after 15 interceptions for the Kansas City Chiefs and the Tampa Bay Buccaneers, and he added 97 yards on kickoff returns. The safety led the 1982 national championship squad with four interceptions and finished second behind Scott Radecic with 70 tackles.

The number of total yards (313) the Nittany Lions amassed in the 1961 Gator Bowl. Georgia Tech totaled 412 total yards, but Penn State won the field position game — with eight punts traveling an average of 41 yards — and took the title as well by a score of 30-15.

The combined number of receiving yards (314) for wide receivers Bobby Engram (169) and Freddie Scott (145) in a 1994 contest against Michigan State. The pass catching duo eclipsed the century mark two other times in the same game that season (Rutgers and Temple).

The number of tackles (315) Brian Gelzheiser made from 1991-94. Gelzheiser was fundamentally sound in space, registering 157 solo tackles, while aiding support to his fellow teammates with 158 assists. The linebacker led the Nittany Lions in tackles in his junior and senior seasons, including a 126-tackle effort during the 1994 undefeated campaign.

The number of kickoff return yards (316) Paul Johnson accounted for during his collegiate career from 1967-69. Johnson returned 12 kickoffs, including a 91-yard touchdown scamper in a 27-3 victory over Colorado early in the 1969 season.

The number of passing yards (317) that came off Kerry Collins' right arm during a 30-17 loss at Brigham Young in 1992. Collins attempted a single game school record 54 passes with 28 completions and one touchdown pass.

The number of receiving yards (318) recorded by tight end Mike McCloskey during his four year NFL career with the Houston Oilers and the Philadelphia Eagles. McCloskey caught a career best 16 passes during his rookie season, and then posted a career high 152 receiving yards during his second campaign in 1982. McCloskey is famous for his catch that wasn't—a 15-yard out of bounds grab (incorrectly ruled a catch) before Todd Blackledge's scoring strike to Kirk Bowman in the victory over Nebraska in 1982. Penn State ran with the fortunate break and eventually won the national championship.

The number of total yards (319) Penn State racked up in the 1959 Liberty Bowl against Alabama. Galen Hall's 18-yard touchdown pass to Roger Kochman in the second quarter held up in a 7-0 victory at Municipal Stadium in Philadelphia.

The number of rushing yards (320) Jim Kerr gained on the ground during the 1959 campaign. Kerr ran for 82 yards on nine carries in Penn State's historic 17-11 victory over Army—its first win over the Cadets in 60 years.

The average yards per punt (32.1) for Vince O'Bara during the 1950 season. O'Bara only punted when he couldn't drive the Nittany Lions into the end zone as the quarterback. He passed for 640 yards and three scores on 38 of 103 passing, and punted 51 times for 1,638 yards.

The number of interception return yards (322) accumulated by Penn State's opponents during the 2004 season. Nittany Lion quarterbacks tossed 19 interceptions, while the defense intercepted 16 passes. Anwar Phillips and Calvin Lowry each totaled four interceptions to lead the team.

The combined number of interceptions and return yards (323) for defensive back Harry Hamilton during his eight-year NFL career with the New York Jets and Tampa Bay Buccaneers. He notched 23 picks and totaled 300 return yards. Hamilton was named a third-team All-American as a senior at Penn State in 1983.

The record number of feet (324) Lynn Bomar tossed a pigskin into the hands of Henry Haines in a publicity stunt set up by New York Giants owner Tim Mara on the 20th floor of New York's American Radiator Corporation. Haines was a three-sport star at Penn State before leading the Giants to the NFL title in 1927 and playing for the world champion New York Yankees as a utility outfielder in 1923.

The number of punt return yards (325) linebacker Dennis Onkotz racked up during the 1969 season. Onkotz continued the building legacy of "Linebacker U" with a 97-tackle performance for the Nittany Lions, one season after intercepting four passes in his first of two All-American campaigns. Yet, Onkotz wasn't a typical Penn State linebacker. He brought his tenacity and talent to special teams, even returning one punt for a touchdown.

The approximate distance in miles (326) between Penn State's campus in University Park, PA, and tackle Negley Norton's hometown of Albany, NY. The four year regular at tackle was in the Pacific Theater in World War II after starting as a freshman in 1944, but he later returned to star for three more years.

The record-setting number of rushing yards (327) turned in by Larry Johnson against Indiana on November 16, 2002. Johnson sprinted past and ran through the Hoosiers to surpass every great running back in Penn State history, compiling a school record 327 yards and four touchdowns in a 58-25 victory. In that game, Johnson moved past Lydell Mitchell for first place on the all-time single-season rushing yards list.

The number of points (32.8) the 1999 Nittany Lions averaged per contest. They outscored their opponents by nearly two touchdowns, yielding just 19.5 points per game. The point differential was even wider before a three-game losing streak to end the season.

The number of yards (329) over the 1,000-yard barrier amassed on the ground by Rodney Kinlaw during the 2007 season. Kinlaw finished the campaign with three consecutive 100-yard games and averaged 5.5 yards per carry on his way to the ninth best single season rushing total in program history.

The number of yards (330) Penn State gained on the ground in the 1997 Fiesta Bowl against Texas. The Nittany Lions rolled on the ground again 10 years later for 270 yards (6.6 yards per carry) in the 2007 Alamo Bowl against Texas A&M for a 24-17 victory.

The number of receiving yards (331) posted by Brad Scovill during the 1979 campaign. Scovill finished with the team leading receiving yardage on 26 catches with three touchdowns.

The number of rushing yards (332) Penn State recorded in a 70-24 victory over Akron on September 4, 1999. The Nittany Lions ran the football 45 times and scored six touchdowns via the ground game.

The grade point average (3.33) of linebacker Gary Gray—one of Joe Paterno's true scholar athletes with a degree in Electrical Engineering. Gray led the team in tackles (115) and interceptions (5) during the 1971 season. The inside linebacker was honored in 1996 by the State College Quarterback Club with the Alumni Achievement Award.

The number of fans (334) over 66,000 in attendance at the 2003 Capital One Bowl between Penn State and Auburn. The Nittany Lions entered the contest with four straight wins and a Heisman Trophy worthy running back, but a stiff breeze negated any passing threat and allowed the Tigers to stack the box against Larry Johnson, who rushed for just 72 yards on 20 carries.

335 The number of receiving yards (335) running back Curt Warner accumulated during Penn State's 1982 national championship season. Warner was remembered for what he accomplished in the backfield that season, rushing for 1,041 yards with 8 touchdowns. However, he also caught 24 passes for 5 touchdowns.

336 The number of yards (336) Penn State surrendered through the air to Arizona State quarterback Dennis Sproul in the 1977 Fiesta Bowl. Penn State quarterback Chuck Fusina completed just 8 of 23 passes for 83 yards, but the running game and 18 tackles from Matt Millen propelled the Nittany Lions to victory.

337 The number of receiving yards (337) for tight end Matt Kranchick during the 2003 season. Zack Mills and Michael Robinson used the tight end's 6' 7" frame on fade routes and down the seam. Kranchick averaged a team best 15.3 yards per catch and scored one touchdown. The Pittsburgh Steelers selected him in the sixth round of the 2004 NFL draft.

338 The combined number of receptions and receiving yards (338) for wide receiver Scott Fitzkee during his brief four year NFL career with the Philadelphia Eagles and the San Diego Chargers. The fifth-round draft choice made 17 grabs good for 321 yards, but he also caught four touchdowns and averaged 18 yards per reception. Fitzkee caught Penn State's lone touchdown of the 1979 Sugar Bowl—a 17-yard strike from Chuck Fusina.

339 The combined number of total offensive yards gained and net rushing yards allowed (339) against Michigan State on November 18, 2006. The Nittany Lion offense tallied 325 total yards—led by Tony Hunt, who rushed for 130 yards—and the Nittany Lion defense gave up just 14 yards rushing on 15 attempts (only 0.9 yards per carry).

340 The number of punt return yards (340) Calvin Lowry gained on 32 punts during 2006. In 2005, Lowry amassed 232 yards on

28 punt returns. The safety also led the team with 26 returns for 240 yards during the 2004 season.

The single-game, all-purpose yards record (341) set by Curt Warner in a 41-16 victory at Syracuse in 1981. Warner's 1981 season was just the tip of the iceberg in a four-year career that ended with a trip to the record books.

The number of carries (342) totaled by running back Mike Guman during his nine-year NFL career with the Los Angeles Rams. Guman's best season was his second, when he amassed a career best 433 yards with four touchdowns. The fullback played in 106 career games with 1,286 yards and 11 scores. He finished as Penn State's leading scorer during his 1976 freshman season with 8 touchdowns for 48 points.

The combined number of receiving yards (343) for Henry Opperman in 1959 and 1960. Opperman caught 11 passes for 212 yards as a junior and hauled in 13 passes for 131 yards and a score in 1960. He was a key member of Rip Engle's first two bowl teams.

The number of kickoff return yards (344) gained by Gary Brown on eight returns during the 1990 season. Brown did most of his damage in a 17-13 loss to Texas in 1990, compiling a single game record 201 kickoff return yards.

The grade point average (3.45) for center Jack Baiorunos in pre-dentistry at Penn State. Baiorunos started at center for two-and-a-half years and was a third-team All-American in 1974.

The number of all-purpose yards (34.6) Chafie Fields averaged per contest during the 1998 season. Fields was used primarily as a pass catcher with 369 receiving yards along with 11 kickoff return yards and one rushing yard.

The team-leading number of receiving yards (347) recorded by Bill Huber during the 1964 campaign. Huber caught 25 passes with one touchdown for the Nittany Lions.

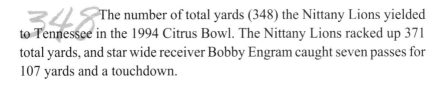

The number of total yards (348) the Nittany Lions yielded to Tennessee in the 1994 Citrus Bowl. The Nittany Lions racked up 371 total yards, and star wide receiver Bobby Engram caught seven passes for 107 yards and a touchdown.

The combined number of games played and interception return yards (349) for defensive back David Macklin through the 2007 NFL season. Macklin played 116 games and posted 233 interception return yards. He was a key member of the Indianapolis Colts secondary from 2000-03 before starting at corner for the Arizona Cardinals from 2004-06. Macklin was an All-Big Ten performer as a Nittany Lion in 1998.

The single-game, total offense record for a junior (350) set by quarterback Kerry Collins in a 1993 contest against Michigan State. Never known for his scrambling ability, Collins actually lost two yards on the ground, but torched the Spartans secondary to the tune of 352 yards passing in a wild 38-37 victory.

The team bowl record for rushing yards (351) piled up against Ohio State in the 1980 Fiesta Bowl. Curt Warner ran for 155 yards on 18 carries and Booker Moore added 76 yards on the ground. Penn State's ground game also accounted for four touchdowns in the victory.

The average number of yards (35.2) traveled each time Art Betts punted the football during the 1951 season. Betts punted 53 times, kicking high placement punts and low, long distance rockets that totaled 1,855 yards.

The number of passing yards (353) Elwood Petchel racked up during the 1947 campaign. Petchel completed just 18 of 38 passes with five touchdowns and three interceptions for the Nittany Lions, who finished with consecutive victories over Holy Cross and Pittsburgh.

The grade point average (3.54) for linebacker Carmen Masciantonio. The 1984 Academic All-American was a backup on the 1982 national championship squad and led the team with 14 tackles in a 1984 Aloha Bowl victory over Washington.

The total number of (355) regular season games played (121) by linebacker Rich Milot and his official NFL playing weight in pounds (234). The former PSU standout played all nine of his NFL seasons with the Washington Redskins and intercepted 13 passes.

The number of passing yards (356) the Penn State defense surrendered to Michigan State signal caller Jeff Smoker during a wild 42-37 victory in East Lansing during the 2001 season. The Nittany Lions trailed 31-21 at the half, but Zack Mills accounted for a passing touchdown and a rushing score sandwiched around a two-yard Eric McCoo touchdown. The Nittany Lions defense allowed just six points in the second half with adjustments that confused Smoker and the MSU passing game.

The combined number of NFL rushing and receiving yards (357) compiled by running back Michael Robinson during the 2006 and 2007 seasons. The former PSU star totaled 237 yards on the ground and 120 after the catch. Robinson was drafted by the San Francisco 49ers for his athletic ability and natural football skills.

The number of rushing yards (358) piled up by running back Larry Johnson during the 2000 season. Johnson was used sparingly during both his sophomore and junior campaigns before exploding onto the national stage during his record-breaking 2002 season.

The number of game minutes (359) offensive/defensive guard Dick Deluca was on the field during the 1956 season. Deluca was in the middle of the action more than any player outside Milt Plum and Billy Kane.

The combined number of career games played and interception return yards (360) for linebacker Ralph Baker with the New York Jets from 1964-74. Baker saw action in 142 professional games and amassed 218 return yards following interceptions. The Lewistown, PA native starred as a linebacker at Penn State, and then took his ball awareness to the professional level, where he intercepted 19 passes and returned two for touchdowns.

The number of total yards (361) Penn State amassed in the 1969 Orange Bowl victory over Kansas. Bob Campbell ran for 101 yards for the Nittany Lions, who looked beaten before the frantic finish. The *Pittsburgh Press* wrote of the finish, "There was no way Penn State could win . . . the last two minutes were pure unadulterated insanity."

The number of rushing yards (362) gained by Penn State running backs Franco Harris, Lydell Mitchell, and Charlie Pittman in a 38-16 victory over Boston College in 1969. Each running back gained over 100 yards—one of just two times in program history a trio of running backs reached the 100-yard mark in the same game. Harris ran for 136 yards, Mitchell sprinted for 120 yards, and Pittman added 106 yards on the ground against Boston College.

The number of passing yards (363) Penn State surrendered during the 1967 Gator Bowl against Florida State. The Nittany Lions managed just 69 yards passing, but outgained the Seminoles 175-55 on the ground. Joe Paterno, coaching in his first bowl game, decided to go for a first down deep in his team's own territory early in the third quarter, but the gamble failed and Florida State used the momentum to eventually force the tie. After the game, Paterno told the *Philadelphia Inquirer*, "I may be rationalizing, but in the long run that fourth down call may be the best thing I ever did for Penn State football."

The completion percentage (36.4) for Tony Sacca in the NFL. Sacca played in just two games for the Phoenix Cardinals, who selected the quarterback in the second round after a productive career in Happy Valley. The signal caller completed just 4 of 11 passes for 29 yards with two interceptions.

The number of receiving yards (365) for wide receiver Eddie Drummond during the 2000 season. Drummond played his first three-plus seasons as a wide receiver before head coach Joe Paterno moved him into the backfield midway through his senior season. Drummond finished his collegiate career with 71 receptions for 1,132 yards along with 272 yards rushing and a score.

The number of passing yards (366) for Mike McQueary in Penn State's 34-17 victory over Pittsburgh in 1997. McQueary's big day set the single game passing yardage record by a senior.

The punting average in yards (36.7) for Ted "The Foot" Kemmerer during the 1952 campaign. Kemmerer punted the football 52 times for 1,904 yards — and his booming kicks helped Penn State upset Pitt and Penn that year.

The number of receiving yards (368) compiled by Corey Jones during the 1998 campaign, one yard behind Chafie Fields for the team lead. Jones did best Fields' 25 catches with 27 of his own to go along with two touchdowns.

The number of carries (369) for quarterback/running back/wide receiver Michael Robinson during his collegiate career. The offensive star began his Penn State career lined up in the backfield and spread out wide before leading Penn State to the 2006 Orange Bowl as the starting quarterback. Robinson became the only Nittany Lion quarterback to rush for more than 1,000 yards as he compiled 1,637 yards and 20 touchdowns from 2002-05.

The number of passes (370) Kerry Collins completed during his decorated collegiate career. Collins threw for 5,304 yards with 39 touchdown passes and just 21 interceptions before taking his rocket right arm to the NFL.

The number of pass completions (371) for Chuck Fusina from 1975-78. Fusina's best season came in 1977 with 2,221 passing yards and 15 touchdowns. He finished his career with 5,382 yards through the air and 37 touchdown passes.

The total number of tackles (372) credited to linebacker Paul Posluszny. The linebacker accumulated 210 solo tackles and 162 assists to outdistance Greg Buttle over a four-year stay in the heart of Penn State's defense from 2003-06.

The team leading rushing total (373) collected by Elwood Petchel during the 1946 campaign. Petchel also led the Nittany Lions with 287 yards passing and 2 touchdowns. On the ground, Petchel averaged five yards per carry and scored seven times.

The team leading number of game minutes (374) played by Milt Plum in 1956. Plum was a successful quarterback and a punter, booming 33 punts for 1,297 yards and a 39.3 yard average.

The average number of punt yards (37.5) traveled off Wayne Corbett's foot in 1966. Corbett punted 63 times in 1996, 19 more than he had in posting a 37.7 yard per punt average the previous season.

The number of total yards (376) Penn State accumulated in the 1972 Cotton Bowl against Texas. John Hufnagel was an efficient 7 of 12 for 137 yards and a touchdown in the victory. Split end Scott Skarzynski and Hufnagel hooked up for a 65-yard touchdown to provide an early cushion.

The number of yards (377) lost on Penn State's 93 tackles behind the line of scrimmage during the 2006 season. Defensive tackle Jay Alford forged the way with 14.5 tackles behind the line of scrimmage. The Nittany Lion trio of tackling machines at linebacker then took over led by: Paul Posluszny with 9.5 tackles for a loss; Dan Connor with 9 tackles behind the line of scrimmage; and Sean Lee with 8 tackles for a loss.

The number of punt return yards (378) totaled by Lenny Moore during his collegiate career. Moore was a threat every time he touched the football, and he used his vision and shifty running style effectively in the return game. Moore returned 13 punts for a career high 228 yards and one touchdown during the 1953 campaign.

The combined number of NFL starts and interception return yards (379) for 1988 Hall of Fame inductee Jack Ham. The heart of Pittsburgh's famed "Steel Curtain" defense intercepted 32 passes in a career that saw him start 161 professional games. He tallied 218 interception return yards and his stellar play earned him eight trips to the

Pro Bowl. Ham served as co-captain for the 1970 Nittany Lions, making 92 tackles and intercepting four passes.

The total number of yards from scrimmage (380) for running back Roger Kochman during his lone NFL season. Kochman ran for 232 yards and caught four passes for 148 yards one touchdown for the Buffalo Bills in 1963. Kochman was a member of the Nittany Lions from 1959-62, starring in the backfield during his final two seasons in Happy Valley.

The number of games (381) coached by defensive coordinator Jerry Sandusky. Penn State sent Sandusky out in style during his last game, holding Texas A&M to 202 total yards and keeping it off the scoreboard in a 24-0 1999 Alamo Bowl victory.

The number of carries (382) for running back Lenny Moore during a three-year stretch from 1953-55. Moore ran for a career best 1,082 yards in 1954 and ended his collegiate career with 2,380 rushing yards and 23 touchdowns.

The number of team high receiving yards (383) posted by John Smidansky during the 1950 season. Smidansky caught 23 passes with three touchdowns for the Nittany Lions, who won their final four games to finish with a respectable 5-3-1 mark.

The average number of yards (38.4) traveled on a Ron Colone punt from 1946-48. Colone served as the Nittany Lions punter for three consecutive seasons, and he averaged a career-high, 40 yards per punt during the 1947 season.

The average number of yards (38.5) Penn State was penalized per game during the 2001 season. The Nittany Lions were penalized 54 times for 424 yards, while their opponents were flagged 67 times for 609 yards (55.4 yards per contest).

The number of receiving yards (386) amassed by Kenny Jackson during his freshman season of 1980. Jackson caught 21 of his 109 career passes during his first season in Happy Valley. He was a starter on teams that had a four-year mark of 39-9-1 with two trips to the Fiesta Bowl and another to the Sugar Bowl.

387 The combined number of rushing and receiving yards (387) for running back Mike Meade during his NFL career. Meade carried the football 72 times and made 21 receptions—good for 261 and 126 yards respectively—for the Green Bay Packers and the Detroit Lions from 1982-85. The running back ran for 60 yards on nine carries during Penn State's dominating victory over Southern California in the 1982 Fiesta Bowl.

388 The number of team-best kickoff return yards (388) racked up by freshman A.J. Wallace during the 2006 season. Wallace returned 16 kickoffs for an average of 24.2 yards per return. Wallace also played cornerback and wide receiver. In the season opener versus Akron, he zipped around the edge for a 42-yard sprint on his first collegiate snap.

389 The average number of yards (38.9) per punt for Bob Parsons during his collegiate career from 1969-71. Parsons used the high altitude of Boulder to boom a 69-yard punt in a 1970 contest at Colorado. He was taken in the fifth round of the 1972 NFL draft by the Chicago Bears—the only team he played for in his 12-year NFL career.

390 The average number of yards (39.0) traveled on a Doug Helkowski punt from 1988-91. Helkowski served as the punter in each of his four collegiate campaigns and averaged a career best 39.4 yards per kick in 1990.

391 The grade point average (3.91) for one of Penn State's great scholar athletes, Bruce Bannon. The defensive end/linebacker was a consensus first-team All-American during his 1972 senior season. Bannon finished his career with 223 tackles and was the fifth choice of the New York Jets in the 1973 NFL draft.

392 The combined number of rushing and receiving yards (392) piled up by fullback Jon Witman during his six-year NFL career with the Pittsburgh Steelers. Witman gained 263 yards on the ground and 129 after the catch. He teamed with fellow fullback Brian Milne to form a powerful one-two blocking punch for the Nittany Lions through the 1995 season.

393 The number of passing yards (393) Don Bailey accumulated in 1954. Bailey completed 33 passes with five touchdowns for the 1954 Nittany Lions, who won their last four games to finish with a 7-2 record.

394 The number of points (394) Penn State scored during the 2007 campaign. The Nittany Lions averaged 30.3 points per contest, but gave up only 228 points for an average of 17.5 points per game.

395 The number of sacks (39.5) recorded by defensive end Bruce Clark during his eight-year NFL career. After terrorizing quarterbacks for Penn State, Clark took his tenacity and pure speed to the NFL where he sacked the quarterback a career best 10.5 times in 1984 for the New Orleans Saints.

396 The number of rushing yards (396) Michael Robinson gained during the 2003 season. Penn State's dynamic offensive threat also threw for 892 yards, pushing his total offensive yards for the season to 1,288. Robinson threw three touchdown passes and ran for five more scores.

397 The average number of yards (39.7) traveled on a Bob Parsons punt during the 1981 season. Parsons' career high 114 punts traveled 4,531 yards in 16 games for the Chicago Bears. Chicago's fifth-round draft choice in 1972 spent his entire 12-year career in the Windy City and flashed back to his days at Penn State by also lining up at tight end. He caught 13 passes for 184 yards and a touchdown for the Bears in 1975.

398 The number of rushing yards (398) gained by Steve Irwin during the 1965 campaign. Irwin played second fiddle to Dave McNaughton on the ground, but the all-purpose back also racked up 217 receiving yards and 359 return yards for the Nittany Lions, who defeated Maryland in their final game to finish with a 5-5 mark.

399 The single-game, passing yards record (399) set by left-hander Zack Mills against Iowa in a wild 42-35 overtime loss in 2002. Penn State rallied from a 22-point deficit to force overtime at Beaver Stadium.

400 The milestone victory (400) obtained with a 17-7 triumph across the country at Oregon on September 21, 1963. Ralph Baker served as team captain and Rip Engle was nearing the end of his tenure as head coach of the Nittany Lions. Penn State won four of its last five games to finish with a 7-3 record.

Penn State Nittany Lions, 1994 Schedule

Opponent	Result
at Minnesota	W 56-3
#14 USC	W 38-14
Iowa	W 61-21
Rutgers	W 55-27
at Temple	W 48-21
at #5 Michigan	W 31-24
#21 Ohio State	W 63-14
at Indiana	W 35-29
at Illinois	W 35-31
Northwestern	W 45-17
Michigan State	W 59-31
vs. #12 Oregon (Rose Bowl)	W 38-20

"Its the name on the front of the jersey that matters most,
not the one on the back."

— Joe Paterno's motto even with the ultra-talented 1994 squad

Chapter Five

The Greatest Show on Manure

In a flash, it was history.
Not to sell the 1994 Penn State football juggernaut short on its lasting impact, for names like Kerry Collins, Ki-Jana Carter, and Kyle Brady will forever be synonymous with college football, but its offensive domination was not surgical in nature.

Scoring drives lasted roughly two minutes, and they took on a systematic approach with large gains piled in succession.

Each march looked identical and ended the same way—with the Nittany Lions in the end zone. Or at least it seemed that way for an offense that averaged a jaw-dropping 47.8 points and 520.2 yards of total offense per contest.

There were few time-consuming, three-yards-and-plenty-of-dust drives that drove Joe Paterno's success during the 1980s. There were plenty of meetings between Carter and opposing safeties—the same safeties Bobby Engram left in his rearview mirror on a post pattern.

In just its second season of Big Ten conference play, Penn State transformed its offensive identity from a methodical, plodding bunch perfectly constructed for the Big Ten style to a contingent of track stars seldom seen in the rough and tough conference.

Many Penn State loyalists slobbered over the game changing athleticism, but wondered whether the shift to speed would play well on a late November day in Ann Arbor or during an early winter snow squall in Madison.

As it turned out, speed worked everywhere. It excelled in the cold and in the rain. It rolled over opponents in the mud and wind. It probably would have scored 50 points on a stretch of manure in nearby Potters Mill.

The Nittany Lions became the first Big Ten squad to earn a 12-0 record and the first conference team to finish off an unbeaten season since Ohio State in 1968. It was a season that included the famed 96-yard drive to cap off a 21-point comeback at Illinois and the last second Hail Mary heave by Indiana that made a blowout seem closer and pushed Penn State permanently off its perch atop the polls.

That season was capped by one more statement, one more mark that defined one of the greatest collegiate offenses ever assembled. Carter took a handoff on Penn State's first play from scrimmage in the 1995 Rose Bowl against Pac Ten representative Oregon, and he headed off tackle for what looked like a four or five yard gain in the making.

That wasn't what Carter saw on his way outside. He bounced off the designated running lane, found space between the over pursuing linebackers and *in a flash, he was history*. Carter's 83-yard mad dash to the end zone was a Run to the Roses and a race to a national championship that eluded the Nittany Lions through no fault of their own.

Carter finished with 156 rushing yards in a 38-20 victory that capped Paterno's fifth unbeaten, untied season, and made him college football's all-time winningest bowl coach with 16 postseason victories. He also became the first head coach to win all four major bowl games—Rose, Orange, Sugar, and Cotton.

Not surprisingly, Penn State eclipsed seven individual and two team school bowl records in the process. The statement had been made, but fell on deaf ears. Nebraska won the national championship, marking the fourth time a Paterno-led team finished unbeaten without a national title.

The lack of championship distinction didn't deter from the milestones Penn State accomplished in its season of offensive firepower. Collins, Carter, Brady, and Engram all contributed to a record-setting offense, and in turn, used their individual successes to provide great opportunities at the next level.

The season was a part of history. Each chapter was typically quick, but the story will remain forever.

The number of passes (401) completed by Tony Sacca during his collegiate career from 1988-91. Sacca threw for 5,869 yards and 41 touchdowns to just 24 interceptions. He threw for a career best 292 yards and one touchdown in a 35-32 loss to Boston College during the 1991 season.

The number of punt return yards (402) amassed by Bobby Engram during the 1993 season. Engram returned 33 punts and averaged 12.2 yards per return. The wide receiver/return specialist also led the team in punt return yardage throughout the 1995 season with 187 yards on 19 returns.

The number of receiving yards (403) for Ted Kwalick during the 1968 season. He led the team with 31 catches and 2 touchdowns. He caught 33 passes for 563 yards and 4 scores one year earlier.

The number of kick return yards (404) racked up by Kevin Baugh during the 1982 season. His speed and vision gave Penn State an extra dimension during the national championship campaign, when he accumulated 315 punt return yards and was a threat on 18 kickoff returns.

The average number of yards per punt (40.5) off the foot of Chris Clauss during the 1987 season. Clauss booted 62 punts for 2,511 yards, including a 76-yard bomb against Rutgers.

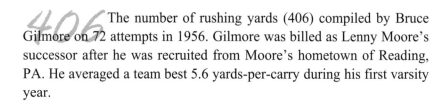

The number of rushing yards (406) compiled by Bruce Gilmore on 72 attempts in 1956. Gilmore was billed as Lenny Moore's successor after he was recruited from Moore's hometown of Reading, PA. He averaged a team best 5.6 yards-per-carry during his first varsity year.

The average number of yards per punt (40.7) off the left foot of Jeremy Kapinos in a 27-25 loss at Michigan in 2005. Penn State's only loss of the season came on the last play of the game, as Wolverines quarterback Chad Henne threw a touchdown pass to Mario Manningham for the victory.

The number of passes (408) attempted by John Hufnagel during his collegiate career from 1970-72. Hufnagel's best season came in 1972, when he threw for 2,039 yards and 15 touchdowns to just eight interceptions.

The average number of yards per punt (40.9) off the foot of John Bruno in 1986. Bruno led the Nittany Lions in punting during three successive seasons, averaging 41.4 yards per kick as a sophomore and 42.9 yards per punt in 1985.

The number of receiving yards (410) for Maurice Humphrey in 2003. Humphrey finished right on the heels of Tony Johnson for the team lead in receptions and yardage, catching 30 passes with one touchdown.

The average number of yards per punt (41.1) for Ralph Giacomarro during the 1982 season. Giacomarro booted 47 punts for 1,933 yards with two blocked punts during his senior campaign.

The number of yards (412) Penn State's defense surrendered in the 1980 Fiesta Bowl. Frank Case won the game's Outstanding Defensive Player award and helped keep Ohio State out of the end zone after halftime.

The number of points (413) Penn State scored during the 2005 season. The Nittany Lions averaged 34.4 points per contest and surrendered 17.7 points per game. Penn State used a strong ground game to churn out victories, averaging 212.8 rushing yards per game to just 93 for its opponents.

The number of rushing yards (414) Blair Thomas racked up over the 1,000-yard barrier during the 1987 season. Thomas also posted 300 yards receiving and 58 yards in the return game for 1,772 all-purpose yards.

The number of catches (415) hauled in by wide receiver O.J. McDuffie during his nine-year NFL career with the Miami Dolphins. The former Penn State All-American caught an NFL-leading 90 passes as Dan Marino's favorite target in 1998. He finished his career with 5,074 receiving yards and 29 receiving scores.

The average number of yards (41.6) traveled on each of the opponent's punts during the 2005 season. Penn State punted just 61 times (23 times fewer than its opponents) for an average of 41.3 yards per kick.

The average number of yards per punt (41.7) for John Bruno, Jr. from 1984-86. Bruno punted 204 times for 8,508 yards and played on the 1986 national championship squad.

The number of total offensive yards (418) Penn State yielded to Florida State during the 1967 Gator Bowl. The Nittany Lions forced four interceptions and saw the Seminoles penalized four times over the course of the contest.

The all-time Penn State record number of tackles (419) made by Dan Connor during his collegiate career. The 2007 Bednarik Award winner also finished his decorated stay in Happy Valley with 34 tackles behind the line of scrimmage, sitting on the same number as fellow star linebacker Paul Posluszny.

The number of total offensive yards (420) piled up by the Nittany Lions in the 1960 Liberty Bowl. Penn State's "Reddie" unit—the second-team offense—scored three 4th quarter touchdowns in the victory over Oregon.

The number of plays (421) the Penn State offense ran with Rashard Casey under center during the 2000 season. Casey led an offense that averaged 22 points and 325.7 yards of total offense per contest.

The combined number of career receptions and receiving yards (422) for tight end Vyto Kab during his five-year NFL career with the Philadelphia Eagles, the New York Giants, and the Detroit Lions. He made 36 grabs in his career for 386 yards. Kab lined up opposite Mike McCloskey and handled most of the dirty work in the trenches for the high octane 1981 Penn State offense.

The combined number of kickoffs returned and kickoff yards (423) for the Nittany Lions against Notre Dame on September 8, 2007. Kevin Kelly boomed two of his six kickoffs for touchbacks as he amassed 420 yards for the Nittany Lions. On the receiving end, the Lions special teams squad returned three kicks, led by A.J. Wallace, who took one for a 68-yard sprint in the 31-10 victory over the Fighting Irish.

The number of kickoff return yards (424) racked up by Shelly Hammonds during the 1993 campaign. Hammonds returned 16 kickoffs for an average of 26.5 yards per return.

The number of rushing yards (425) totaled by Bob Pollard in 1951. Pollard carried the football 57 times for a 7.5-yard average. He sprinted for 243 yards on just 14 carries with touchdown runs of 75 and 71 yards against Rutgers in the next to last game of the season.

The number of passing yards (426) for quarterback Richie Lucas during the 1957 campaign. Lucas also rushed for 66 yards and threw four touchdown passes.

The number of kickoff return yards (427) piled up by Gary Brown during the 1988 season. The running back returned 22 kickoffs for a 19.4-yard average.

The combined winning percentage (.428) of the Big Ten's bowl teams following the 2005 regular season. Penn State joined Ohio State and Wisconsin as the three victorious clubs in seven postseason games.

The number of passing yards (429) compiled by Mike Cooper during the 1970 season. Cooper completed 32 of 64 passes with four touchdowns and six interceptions.

The number of total offensive yards (430) Penn State's high-powered offense piled up in the 1995 Rose Bowl. Ki-Jana Carter dashed 83 yards for a touchdown on Penn State's first play from scrimmage and finished the contest with 156 rushing yards and two other touchdowns.

The average number of yards per game (431) for Purdue's offense going into a November 3, 2007, contest at Penn State. The Nittany Lion defense held the Boilermakers to 323 total yards in a 26-19 victory.

The number of points (432) scored by the 1991 Nittany Lions. Tony Sacca led the high-powered offense, while an opportunistic defense and above average special teams helped lead the team to a 36 points-per-game average and an 11-2 record.

The number of receiving yards (43.3) wide receiver Kenny Jackson averaged per contest during his 1985 season with the Philadelphia Eagles. The wide receiver finished with a career high 40 catches for 692 yards during his second professional season in 1985.

The average number of yards per punt (43.4) for John Bruno during the 1987 Fiesta Bowl. Bruno is best known for his booming kicks that maintained Penn State's field position advantage against the Miami Hurricanes.

The total number of sacks and games played (43.5) by defensive end Larry Kubin during his brief NFL career. Kubin played only 43 NFL games and recorded 0.5 sacks, but he got to play for the

1982 Super Bowl champion Washington Redskins after a decorated stay in Happy Valley, where he earned the nickname "Mr. Sackman" after totaling 30 sacks from 1977-80.

436 The number of team-leading rushing yards (436) compiled by Austin Scott during the 2003 season. Scott actually had seven fewer carries than quarterback/running back Michael Robinson, but he outdistanced the versatile playmaker with 4.4 yards per carry and five touchdowns.

437 The number of passes (437) attempted by Penn State's opponents during the 2007 campaign. The Nittany Lions defense intercepted 11 of those attempts with safety Anthony Scirrotto picking off a team-best three passes.

438 The combined number of rushing attempts and rushing touchdowns (438) recorded by Steve Smith during his nine-year NFL career with the Oakland Raiders and the Seattle Seahawks. Smith tallied 429 attempts and nine touchdowns, but he primarily served as a lead blocker. A co-captain on the 1986 national championship team, Smith finished his Penn State career with 1,246 rushing yards and 11 touchdowns.

439 The number of total yards (439) Penn State's defensive unit sent opponents in the wrong direction on 102 tackles behind the line of scrimmage in 2007. Maurice Evans accounted for 21.5 of those tackles and Dan Connor added 15.

440 The number of receiving yards (440) accumulated by Derrick Williams during the 2006 campaign. Williams hauled in 40 passes with one touchdown during his sophomore season.

441 The number of total offensive yards (441) Penn State's defense gave up in the 1999 Outback Bowl against Kentucky. Penn State's defense bent but didn't break, allowing Tim Couch to throw for 336 yards on a staggering 48 attempts. Kevin Thompson didn't pile up the style points, but he protected the football and threw for 187 yards with one touchdown in Penn State's eighth straight January bowl game.

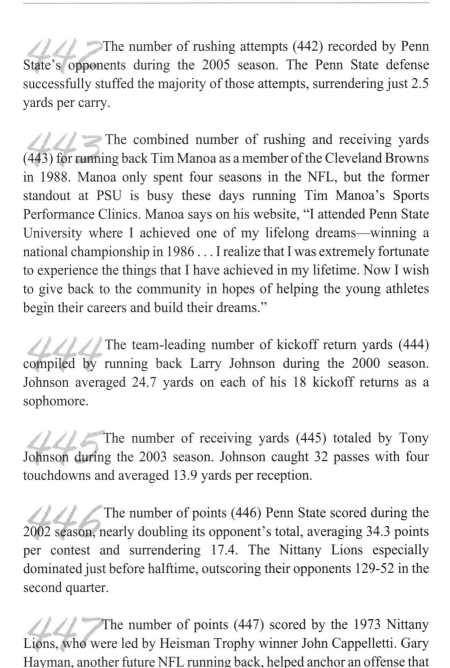

The number of rushing attempts (442) recorded by Penn State's opponents during the 2005 season. The Penn State defense successfully stuffed the majority of those attempts, surrendering just 2.5 yards per carry.

The combined number of rushing and receiving yards (443) for running back Tim Manoa as a member of the Cleveland Browns in 1988. Manoa only spent four seasons in the NFL, but the former standout at PSU is busy these days running Tim Manoa's Sports Performance Clinics. Manoa says on his website, "I attended Penn State University where I achieved one of my lifelong dreams—winning a national championship in 1986 . . . I realize that I was extremely fortunate to experience the things that I have achieved in my lifetime. Now I wish to give back to the community in hopes of helping the young athletes begin their careers and build their dreams."

The team-leading number of kickoff return yards (444) compiled by running back Larry Johnson during the 2000 season. Johnson averaged 24.7 yards on each of his 18 kickoff returns as a sophomore.

The number of receiving yards (445) totaled by Tony Johnson during the 2003 season. Johnson caught 32 passes with four touchdowns and averaged 13.9 yards per reception.

The number of points (446) Penn State scored during the 2002 season, nearly doubling its opponent's total, averaging 34.3 points per contest and surrendering 17.4. The Nittany Lions especially dominated just before halftime, outscoring their opponents 129-52 in the second quarter.

The number of points (447) scored by the 1973 Nittany Lions, who were led by Heisman Trophy winner John Cappelletti. Gary Hayman, another future NFL running back, helped anchor an offense that churned out yards on the ground. The Nittany Lions averaged 40.6 points per game on their way to an unbeaten 12-0 season.

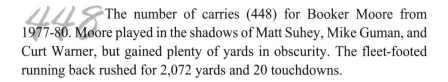

448 The number of carries (448) for Booker Moore from 1977-80. Moore played in the shadows of Matt Suhey, Mike Guman, and Curt Warner, but gained plenty of yards in obscurity. The fleet-footed running back rushed for 2,072 yards and 20 touchdowns.

449 The number of interception return yards (449) accumulated by linebacker Dave Robinson during his 12-year professional career. Robinson intercepted 27 passes with one touchdown. The member of Linebacker U was Penn State's first black All-American with his selection to the team in 1962.

450 The team-best number of rushing yards (450) for Gary Klingensmith during the 1963 season. Klingensmith carried the football 102 times, averaging 4.4 yards per carry with three touchdowns. The Nittany Lions finished the season ranked 16th in the country by UPI with a 7-3 record.

451 The number of receiving yards (451) racked up by tight end Tony Stewart during the 2000 season. Stewart lived up to the hype as an athletic offensive presence that stretched defenses down the seam as a high school star at Allentown Central Catholic. He caught 38 passes with two touchdowns as a collegiate senior to become the first tight end since 1979 to lead the team in receiving.

452 The number of rushing yards (452) Penn State's defense surrendered to Michigan State in the 1997 regular season finale. The Nittany Lions yielded just 3.8 yards per carry to Ron Dayne and the rest of the Wisconsin running backs just one week earlier in a 35-10 victory, but the defensive unit was unable to repeat that success against the Spartans as they suffered a 49-14 drumming on the road.

453 The number of total offensive yards (453) Penn State's defense allowed to Oklahoma in the 1972 Sugar Bowl. Penn State forced eight fumbles (recovering five) against a powerful wishbone attack to stay in the game despite gaining only 196 total yards.

The number of carries (454) for running back Charlie Pittman from 1967-69. The workhouse led the Nittany Lions in rushing each season, compiling a career best 950 yards and 14 touchdowns during the 1968 campaign. Pittman is one of just nine running backs to lead the team in rushing at least three straight seasons, but he was the first to achieve the honor since Lenny Moore from 1953-55.

The number of passing yards (455) Akron quarterback Luke Getsy piled up in the 2005 Motor City Bowl against Memphis, his last game before the Penn State defense held him to 160 yards passing with two interceptions in the 2006 season opener. Anthony Morelli had more success under center, throwing three touchdown passes in a 34-16 victory over the Akron Zips.

The number of carries (456) for Curtis Enis during his brief three-year NFL career. Enis gained 1,497 yards on the ground with four rushing scores. He also caught 45 passes for 340 yards and two more touchdowns for the Chicago Bears. He tore the ACL in his left knee during his rookie season, which contributed to the brevity of his career.

The number of rushing attempts (457) by the Nittany Lions during the 2006 season. Tony Hunt handled well over half of that number with 277 carries for 1,386 yards and 11 touchdowns.

The number of receiving yards (45.8) Tony Johnson averaged per contest during the 2001 season. Johnson caught 27 passes for 504 yards and three touchdowns.

The number of penalty yards (459) Penn State's Big Ten counterpart Minnesota racked up during the 2003 season—the second highest total in the Big Ten. By comparison, the Nittany Lions were the least penalized team in the conference with just 26 penalties for 178 yards.

The number of passes (460) completed by quarterback Anthony Morelli during his Nittany Lion career. The signal caller had

822 pass attempts, good for 5,275 yards and 31 touchdowns. Morelli is tied for third in program history with 11 career 200-yard passing games.

The number of kickoff return yards (461) totaled by Jon Williams during his 1984 season with the New England Patriots. Williams was overshadowed by Curt Warner during his collegiate career, yet still managed to roll up 2,042 career rushing yards and 14 touchdowns from 1980-83.

The number of passes (462) tight end Mickey Shuler caught during his 14-year NFL career with the New York Jets and the Philadelphia Eagles. Shuler's best statistical season came in 1985, when he caught a career high 76 passes for 879 yards and seven touchdowns with the Jets. Shuler was a three-year letterman at Penn State from 1975-77.

The AP ranking and year (#4, '63) of Pittsburgh in 1963 when PSU met up with the Panthers at Pitt Stadium. Penn State came home with a 22-21 loss to finish the season.

The number of career NFL receiving yards (464) compiled by tight end Tony Stewart through 2007. The two-year starter at Penn State earned honorable mention All-American recognition by *Football News* as a senior. He then took his game to the next level, beginning his career with the Philadelphia Eagles in 2001. He spent the next five seasons with the Cincinnati Bengals before signing with the Oakland Raiders as a free agent in March 2007.

The number of total offensive yards (465) Penn State averaged per contest going into the November 9, 1997 contest against Michigan at Beaver Stadium. The Big Ten's top offense was shut down throughout the overcast November afternoon, dropping a 34-8 decision to the Wolverines. Penn State was held to 169 yards, its lowest offensive output in a defeat in 17 years. The margin was the biggest home defeat in head coach Joe Paterno's 32 seasons (later matched by the Miami Hurricanes' victory in Happy Valley during the 2001 season).

466 The AP ranking and year (#4, '66) of UCLA in 1966 when PSU met up with the Bruins at Los Angeles Memorial Coliseum. It was Joe Paterno's first season at the helm, and Penn State suffered a big loss, 49-11. The Lions closed out the year at 5-5.

467 The combined number of regular season games played and interception return yards (467) by defensive back Mike Zordich during his NFL career from 1987-98. Zordich played for the New York Jets, the Phoenix Cardinals, and the Philadelphia Eagles during his 12-year career. He tallied 282 interception return yards during 185 regular season games. The defensive back was an All-American at Penn State in 1985, when he was credited with 60 tackles as the strong safety.

468 The total number of offensive yards (468) the Nittany Lions accumulated in the 1980 Fiesta Bowl. The offense totaled 22 first downs, but was penalized just twice for ten yards in the victory over Ohio State.

469 The number of rushing yards (469) accumulated by Dave Kasperian during the 1957 season. Kasperian carried the football 122 times with eight touchdowns and made All-East and Honorable Mention All-American. He rushed for 381 yards with seven scores and caught nine passes for 107 yards and two more touchdowns as a senior in 1958.

470 The number of rushing attempts (470) by the Nittany Lions during the 1998 campaign. Eric McCoo and Cordell Mitchell racked up the yards, but fullback Mike Cerimele found the end zone a team best eight times.

471 The number of solo tackles (471) credited to Dan Connor, Sean Lee, and the rest of the Penn State defense during the 2007 season. Connor and Lee were always around the football, finishing with 69 and 54 solo stops respectively. Third on the list was cornerback Lydell Sargeant, a track star and raw athlete who traveled from Lompoc, California to central Pennsylvania to play for the iconic Joe Paterno.

472 The number of receiving yards (472) racked up by Jordan Norwood during the 2006 season. His father, Brian, was the Penn State safeties coach for seven seasons before taking the defensive coordinator position at Baylor. Jordan quickly became a fan favorite because of his local ties (he grew up in State College) and reliable hands. He caught 45 passes with two touchdowns in 2006.

473 The month and year (4, '73) that the 39th annual Sugar Bowl Classic was awarded to Penn State after the University of Oklahoma was forced to forfeit the game played four months earlier because of recruiting violations at OU. The investigation was launched by the Big Eight Conference.

474 The number of rushing yards (474) Curt Warner gained in four bowl games as a Nittany Lion. Warner carried the football 76 times and scored five touchdowns.

475 The number of return yards (475) O.J. McDuffie piled up during the 1991 season. The multitalented McDuffie was a return specialist and offensive and defensive standout in high school at the Hawken School. He set an unofficial Ohio state record with a 108-yard interception return against Wellsville in 1986.

476 The number of punting yards (476) Jeremy Kapinos amassed over the 10,000-yard mark during his solid collegiate career. Kapinos' left foot struck the football 251 times for a 41.7-yard average. His best collegiate contest came in a Big Ten battle against Purdue during the 2004 season, when he rocketed five punts a total of 260 yards (an average of 52 yards per kick) at Beaver Stadium.

477 The average number of yards per punt (47.7) for Greg Reynolds in the 1983 Aloha Bowl, giving Penn State the field possession advantage in a 13-10 victory over Washington. Reynolds' kicking success was highlighted by a 50-yard boot and a deft kick that landed at the Huskies six-yard line late in the 3rd quarter. His performance earned him Defensive Player of the Game honors.

478 The average number of points per game (47.8) the dynamic 1994 Nittany Lions offense scored with Jeff Hartings on the offensive line. Hartings paved the way for an offense that averaged 520.2 yards per game in total offense. In 1995, he joined wide receiver Bobby Engram as the first two Nittany Lions to earn All-Big Ten honors three times.

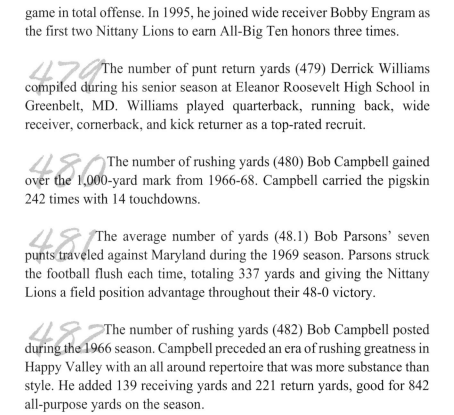

The number of punt return yards (479) Derrick Williams compiled during his senior season at Eleanor Roosevelt High School in Greenbelt, MD. Williams played quarterback, running back, wide receiver, cornerback, and kick returner as a top-rated recruit.

The number of rushing yards (480) Bob Campbell gained over the 1,000-yard mark from 1966-68. Campbell carried the pigskin 242 times with 14 touchdowns.

The average number of yards (48.1) Bob Parsons' seven punts traveled against Maryland during the 1969 season. Parsons struck the football flush each time, totaling 337 yards and giving the Nittany Lions a field position advantage throughout their 48-0 victory.

The number of rushing yards (482) Bob Campbell posted during the 1966 season. Campbell preceded an era of rushing greatness in Happy Valley with an all around repertoire that was more substance than style. He added 139 receiving yards and 221 return yards, good for 842 all-purpose yards on the season.

The number of receiving yards (483) Kenny Jackson posted during the 1983 season. Jackson ended his record-setting career with 28 catches and seven touchdowns during his senior season.

The average number of yards (48.4) Ralph Giacomarro's five punts traveled against the Miami Hurricanes in 1980. Giacomarro's punts traveled a combined distance of 242 yards in the 27-12 victory.

The number of rushing yards (485) Roger Kochman gained over the 1,000-yard mark from 1959-62. Kochman's number was called 264 times, and he delivered 12 rushing touchdowns.

The draft round number and the year (4, '86) that Penn State linebacker Rogers Alexander was selected by the New York Jets in the 1986 NFL draft as the 105th overall selection.

487 The number of total offensive yards (487) Penn State piled up in a 43-14 rout of Auburn in the 1996 Outback Bowl. Wally Richardson threw four touchdown passes and Bobby Engram totaled 113 receiving yards with two touchdowns.

488 The average number of punt yards (48.8) traveled on an opponent's punt during the 2000 season. Rod Perry returned 14 of those punts, Kenny Watson ran back six, and Bruce Branch followed his blockers on five returns.

489 The number of receiving yards (489) Bob Parsons compiled during the 1971 season. Parsons caught 30 passes with five touchdowns for a 15.6-yard-per-catch average. Joe Paterno stated that Parsons had "great speed for his size and naturally soft hands."

490 The combined number of catches/receiving yards (490) for tight-end Dan Natale during the 1972 season. He compiled 460 yards on 30 catches that year and finished his collegiate career with 67 receptions for 1,038 yards and 8 touchdowns, a 15.5 yards-per-catch average.

491 The total number of offensive yards (491) Penn State accumulated during a 41-20 victory over Baylor in the 1975 Cotton Bowl. The school bowl record was largely achieved during the Nittany Lions' 38-point second half explosion, which included a 24-point 4th quarter that sealed their 10th victory of the season.

492 The number of yards per carry (4.92) for fullback Tim Manoa during his stay in Happy Valley. Manoa rushed for 1,098 yards and five touchdowns, with one of those scores accounting for Penn State's lone touchdown in the 1986 Orange Bowl against Oklahoma.

493 The number of return yards (493) compiled by Curt Warner during the 1979 campaign. Warner began his four-year trek into the Penn State record book with 391 rushing yards, 129 receiving yards, and 1,013 all-purpose yards as a freshman.

494 The number of passing yards (494) Purdue quarterback Drew Brees compiled one week before Penn State's defense held him to

361 yards in the Nittany Lions' 31-13 victory during the 1998 season. Courtney Brown sacked Brees three times, and the defense didn't allow a completion of more than 19 yards.

495 The number of career passes (495) attempted by Kevin Thompson as a Penn State quarterback from 1996-99. Thompson completed 263 passes for 3,710 yards, 19 touchdowns, and 17 interceptions. His best season came in 1998 when he threw for 1,691 yards with eight touchdowns and six interceptions.

496 The combined number of NFL receptions and rushing yards (496) for Sam Gash during a solid 12-year career with the New England Patriots, the Buffalo Bills, and the Baltimore Ravens. He caught 169 passes and tallied 327 yards on the ground. Gash was a vital part of Penn State's offense as a senior, serving as the offensive captain and rushing for 391 yards and three scores on 87 carries.

497 The number of carries (497) by Eric McCoo from 1998-2001. McCoo ran for 2,518 yards and 18 touchdowns to hang just outside the top ten on the program's career rushing list.

498 The number of fans (498) over the 97,000 spectator mark on hand to watch Penn State host Michigan in November 1997. The 97,498 fans were the most packed into Beaver Stadium before an 11,000 seat expansion to the south end zone awaited fans during the 2001 campaign.

499 The number of total offensive yards (499) Penn State allowed to the Clemson Tigers in the 1988 Citrus Bowl. Penn State senior linebacker Trey Bauer made six stops and recorded one sack to earn the team's Defensive MVP award.

500 The milestone triumph (500) achieved in a home contest against Ohio University on November 16, 1974. The 35-16 victory pushed the Nittany Lions halfway to a major program milestone of 1,000 victories. Tom Donchez scored three times to help Penn State overcome four lost fumbles.

Robbie Gould, NFL Stats (2005-07)

Year	Team	Games	FGA	FGM	FG%	XPA	XPM	XP%
2005	Chicago	13	27	21	77.8	20	19	95.0
2006	Chicago	16	36	32	88.9	47	47	100.0
2007	Chicago	16	36	31	86.1	33	33	100.0
Career		**45**	**99**	**84**	**84.8**	**100**	**99**	**99.0**

"If God isn't a Penn State fan,
why is the sky blue and white?"

—Penn State bumper sticker

Chapter Six

Robbie's Ultimate Fan

ho thought Robbie Gould would make a Chicago franchise-record 26 straight field goals? Who thought he would drill a 49-yard field goal to push the Bears past Seattle in the 2006 NFC Divisional Playoff? Who even thought he would ever visit Hawaii for anything other than a vacation?

James Weldon did.

And before lifelong football fans flip through their Nittany Lion encyclopedia or even sneak a peak at the remainder of this book's content, let it be known that Weldon never put on shoulder pads or the nationally recognized blue and white jersey.

Unless of course he was masquerading as Zack Mills in an attempt to score with the ladies.

Weldon was as much a member of Nittany Lion nation as Mills, Larry Johnson, or Michael Haynes. He attended Pennsylvania's landmark university from 2001-05 by way of New Hampshire's wooded landscape.

No, Joe Paterno didn't make recruiting trips to Manchester and Concord. Though Weldon did once run into Paterno on his way to a study session.

Weldon was an Economics major. But for the purpose of this dissertation in the history of Penn State football, he was Robbie Gould's ultimate fan.

Even in the dark days at the early part of this decade, Weldon showed up each Saturday to support his favorite player with the rallying cry, "Let's go Robbbbbbie!"

Gould was a walk-on from nearby Lock Haven—a stone's throw from the home of the Little League World Series in Williamsport and perhaps the length of a kickoff from Penn State's main campus. In that way, he was associated with the university from birth and perhaps even dreamed of one day playing for Penn State.

That's just a guess, because well, playing for Penn State is a popular dream for children from the coal regions to the slate quarries. Gould racked up three varsity letters in football and soccer at Central Mountain High School, following a trail blazed by his father Robert, who played professional soccer for the St. Louis Steamers from 1980-83.

Gould took his wiry frame and rocket right foot to Penn State and made a fashionable first impression, earning the regular kicking duties by the fourth game of the season. He made 6 of 10 field goals and finished second to Eric McCoo in scoring.

Few took notice. Weldon was one of those few, cheering on Gould's extra point attempts and booming kicks, which became the status quo by his senior season.

He improved his accuracy as a sophomore, making 17 of 22 field goals with a pair of connections from 50-plus yards. He again finished second in scoring, this time to Larry Johnson's record shattering season.

Johnson's run into the record books soaked up most of the attention. Gould was still just a kicker, a stigma far too often attached to a football player who doesn't normally participate in the game's basic functions (run, throw, catch, or hit).

He struggled with his mechanics at times during the 2003 campaign, making just 9 of 16 attempts but still converting on each of his seven tries from 39 yards and in. He was the inconsistent scoring leader of an inconsistent football team, and some fans became frustrated with everything from run blocking to the kicking game.

Not Weldon, a student so equipped with miniscule facts about Gould's percentages that his friends thought he was serving as the kicker's late night holder instead of cramming for a mid-term exam.

As a senior, Gould was the first player fans saw either after the opening coin toss or following Bobbie Jo's halftime baton twirl. He morphed into a kickoff specialist with a chronically erratic right leg (7 of 13 on field goals in 2004).

After the season, Gould faded into the routine of a normal student. He studied, partied on weekends, and officiated intramural basketball. It was there—on the court, not at the frat—that Weldon came face to face with his football hero for the first time in four years.

He briefly shook Gould's hand and explained his appreciation for the placekicker's accomplishments. He also emphatically stated, "You will be great in the NFL."

The NFL? Any rational person knew that a 55% field goal kicker over his final two seasons wasn't playing at the highest level.

Life, and Weldon, had a different opinion. Gould was signed as an undrafted free agent by New England in late April 2005, and though he spent only four months with the Patriots, he was watching and learning from Adam Vinatieri during that time. He hung around with Baltimore for less than a month before injuries forced the Bears' hand in October. He made 21 of 27 field goals and became the first rookie to lead the proud franchise in scoring since Paul Edinger in 2000.

His professional career had begun. He later made 26 straight field goals, earned All-Pro recognition, and packed his bags for Hawaii and the Pro Bowl.

The impossible had in fact become possible. He pointed to hard work and the support of his teammates, family, friends, and coaches at every level as the reasons for his success.

Others pointed in a different direction. They pointed at Gould's ultimate fan, James Weldon.

501 The number of total offensive yards (501) Penn State surrendered to the Oregon Ducks in the 1995 Rose Bowl. Despite allowing 456 yards through the air, the Nittany Lions' balanced offense and opportunistic defense paved the way to victory. Penn State became the first Big Ten squad to finish with a 12-0 record and the first conference team to earn an unblemished mark since Ohio State in 1968.

502 The number of solo tackles (502) credited to Penn State's opponents during the 2005 season. The Penn State defense totaled 520 solo tackles with linebacker Paul Posluszny registering 64 and safety Chris Harrell racking up 50 solo stops.

503 The single season record (at the time) for kickoff return yards (503) accumulated by Kevin Baugh in 1983. Baugh also held the career mark with 1,216 yards on 62 returns before Kenny Watson jumped to the top of the statistical charts in the late 1990s.

504 The number of rushing yards (504) racked up by Blair Thomas during the 1986 season. Thomas was a change of pace back with just 60 carries. He scored on five of those touches though during his sophomore season.

505 The number of passes (505) attempted by Michael Robinson during his collegiate career. Robinson completed 248 passes for 3,531 yards, 23 touchdowns, and 21 interceptions.

506 The number of receiving yards (506) piled up by Greg Edmonds during the 1970 season. Edmonds led the club in receptions in both 1969 and 1970, but he caught only 20 passes for 246 yards in 1969, and no touchdowns. In 1970, Edmonds caught 38 passes, good for 506 yards and six touchdowns.

507 The number of receiving yards (507) totaled by Jimmy Cefalo during the 1977 campaign. Cefalo compiled a team best 872 all-purpose yards, with 293 return yards and 72 yards via the ground game.

The number of carries (508) Steve Shuey logged from 1977-79. Shuey led the Nittany Lions in rushing each season, totaling a career best 973 yards with six touchdowns in 1979. The model of consistency in the backfield scored 21 touchdowns over the three-year stretch.

The game and year (5, '09) in which PSU beat Bucknell on the road 33-0 on its way to a 5-0-2 record for the year. The PSU defense posted shutouts in all five victories that season: Grove City (31-0), Geneva (46-0), Bucknell (33-0), West Virginia (40-0), and Pittsburgh (5-0). The defense gave up only 11 points all year, which resulted in two ties: Carlisle (8-8) and Pennsylvania (3-3).

The combined number of rushing yards, interceptions, and interception return yards (510) for two-way player Chuck Drazenovich during his ten-year professional career with the Washington Redskins. He posted 330 rushing yards, 15 interceptions, and 165 interception return yards. Drazenovich was the first noted star of aptly named "Linebacker U" to star in the professional ranks.

The completion percentage (51.1) of opposing quarterbacks against the Nittany Lions during the 1999 season. By comparison, Kevin Thompson, Rashard Casey, and Matt Senneca completed 57.1% of their passes.

The number of fans (512) over 42,000 in attendance for Penn State's 38-35 victory at Northwestern in 2001. The Nittany Lions' first win of the season included 213 yards and three scores via the ground game.

The number of rushing yards (513) Evan Royster accumulated on the ground during the 2007 season. Royster's playing time grew after the suspension of Austin Scott, and the freshman responded with 82 attempts, a 6.3 yard average, and 5 touchdowns.

The average yards per punt (51.4) by Jeremy Boone during the 2007 Alamo Bowl. The average broke the program's bowl record of 51.0 yards per kick set by Chris Clauss in the 1988 Citrus Bowl.

515 The completion percentage (51.5) of quarterbacks Rashard Casey and Matt Senneca during the 2000 campaign. Casey handled the majority of the snaps with Senneca throwing just 46 passes on the season.

516 The game and year (5, '16) Penn State was undefeated until it suffered a 15-0 defeat to rival Penn on October 21, 1916. The Lions finished the season with a record of 8-2.

517 The number of wins and year (5, '17) for the Nittany Lions under head coach Dick Harlow. The team finished the season with a 5-4 mark.

518 The number of votes (518) Joe Paterno received in winning the Maxwell Football Club 1994 College Coach of the Year Award. Paterno outdistanced Nebraska head coach Tom Osborne's 216 votes, but Osborne's Cornhuskers won the national championship instead of the unbeaten Nittany Lions.

519 The number of rushing carries (519) for John Cappelletti during his collegiate career. Cappelletti was Penn State's workhouse in 1972 and 1973, proving to be both reliable and productive in the backfield.

520 The number of career receiving yards over the 1,000-yard barrier (520) racked up by Freddie Scott through 1995. Scott played alongside stars Bobby Engram and Kyle Brady on the undefeated 1994 team. The wide receiver finished his career with 93 catches and 11 touchdowns.

521 The number of total offensive yards (521) quarterback Owen Dougherty accumulated during the 1949 season. Dougherty followed in the footsteps of Elwood Petchel under center, piling up the team-leading yardage on 81 plays with five touchdowns.

522 The number of kickoff return yards (522) totaled by Kenny Watson in 1999. Watson returned 22 kickoffs for an average of 23.7 yards per return. In his career, the kickoff return specialist returned the most kickoffs in program history (67) for the most yards (1,506).

The number of solo tackles (523) credited to the Penn State defense during the 2003 season. Yaacov Yisrael led the way with 57 solo tackles and linebacker Gino Capone was right behind with 49 solo stops.

The approximate number of miles (524) between Penn State's campus in University Park, Pennsylvania and Raycom Sports' main offices in Charlotte, North Carolina. Former Nittany Lion defensive tackle Dave Rowe worked as a lead SEC football analyst with the network (formerly known as Lincoln Financial Sports and Jefferson-Pilot Sports) from 1995-2006. Rowe starred on Rip Engle's last team in 1965 and Joe Paterno's first team in 1966 before beginning a lengthy professional career with five different teams.

The number of penalty yards (525) amassed by the 1998 Nittany Lions for an average of just 47.7 yards per game. Their opponents averaged 55.4 penalty yards per contest.

The single season points record (526) set during the 1994 season. The Nittany Lions scored the 526 points in 11 games, and set single season records for touchdowns scored (71), rushing touchdowns (45), and passing scores (23).

The number of rushing attempts (527) for Penn State during the 1947 season. The Nittany Lions totaled 2,713 yards on the ground with 33 touchdowns. Fran Rogel led a well-balanced ground game that averaged 5.1 yards per carry.

The number of passing yards (528) Bob Szanja accounted for in 1951. Szanja completed 41 of 86 passes with three touchdowns. The 1951 Nittany Lions beat Syracuse and Rutgers on their way to a 5-4 season.

The number of receiving yards (529) piled up by Derrick Williams during the 2007 season. Williams caught a team best 55 passes with three touchdowns. Williams also ran for 101 yards and another score.

The game and year (5, '30) Penn State was undefeated until it suffered a severe 40-0 thrashing from Colgate on October 25, 1930. It could not have been much worse, seeing as the loss occurred during the Lions' Homecoming celebration. Penn State finished the season with a 3-4-2 record.

The number of total offensive yards (531) recorded by running back Evan Royster during the 2007 season. The Fairfax, VA freshman was the team's second leading rusher with 513 yards. He added to his rushing total with 18 receiving yards.

The number of losses and year (5, '32) for Penn State in 1932. The team managed only two victories—against Lebanon Valley in the season opener and Sewanee in its final home game of the season—to finish with a disappointing 2-5 mark.

The number of total offensive yards (533) Penn State racked up in a victory over Virginia on November 9, 2002. Zack Mills completed 19 of 30 passes for 227 yards and two touchdowns, with the motivation stemming from the previous season's loss to the Cavaliers. "I played pretty bad the last time we played them," said Mills after the contest, "so it felt pretty sweet to play well today."

The number of yards (534) John Shaffer threw for during the 1984 season. Shaffer played behind Doug Strang and completed only 40 of 96 passes, with seven interceptions to just one touchdown.

The number of all-purpose yards over the 1,000-yard plateau (535) piled up by Blair Thomas during the 1989 season. Thomas added to his team-leading rushing total with 118 receiving yards and 76 return yards.

The number of rushing yards (536) Penn State piled up on the Maryland defense in a 70-7 rout of the Terrapins in 1993. Ki-Jana Carter totaled 159 of those yards, scoring on runs of 63, 36, and 4 yards.

537 The number of kickoff return yards (537) Penn State's opponents totaled on 31 returns during the 2000 season. The Nittany Lions racked up 894 kickoff return yards on 42 returns.

538 The field goal percentage (53.8) for Robbie Gould during the 2004 season. Gould made just 7 of 13 field goals, but he did connect on 22 of 23 extra points for a team high 43 points scored.

539 The number of total offensive yards (539) Penn State accumulated in a 44-14 thumping of Minnesota on October 1, 2005 at Beaver Stadium. The Nittany Lions' attack included 35 first downs, 364 rushing yards, and one ferocious hit from its starting quarterback. Michael Robinson lowered his shoulder and knocked Golden Gophers strong safety Brandon Owens out cold with a scoreboard-worthy punishment early in the second quarter.

540 The number of return yards (540) totaled by Calvin Lowry during the 2003 season. Lowry racked up 240 punt return yards and 300 kickoff return yards for the Nittany Lions.

541 The number of penalty yards (541) racked up by Penn State during the 2000 season. Penn State's opponents were penalized slightly more, totaling 585 yards for an average of 48.8 yards per game.

542 The number of kickoff return yards (542) compiled by Penn State's special teams in 2004. The Nittany Lions returned 31 kickoffs, with running back Rodney Kinlaw taking back a team leading 10 kickoffs for 198 yards.

543 The number of penalty yards (543) amassed by then unbeaten Penn State before its three game slide to end the 1999 regular season. The Nittany Lions were penalized 53 times through nine games, including 13 penalties in a 27-7 victory at Illinois on October 30. "We're still not the smartest team in the world," head coach Joe Paterno scoffed in the ultimate sign of foreshadowing. Penn State dropped a 24-23 decision to Minnesota the following Saturday.

The number of rushing yards (544) compiled by Billy Kane during the 1956 season. Kane averaged 5.0 yards per carry and scored seven touchdowns for the 6-2-1 Nittany Lions.

The number of solo tackles (545) credited to Penn State's opponents during the 2006 season. Penn State tallied 502 solo tackles with Dan Connor registering 70 and fellow "Linebacker U" teammate Paul Posluszny right behind with 69.

The number of all-purpose yards (546) recorded by freshman A.J. Wallace during the 2006 campaign. The cornerback was a threat on all sides of the ball with 388 kickoff return yards, 153 rushing yards, and 5 receiving yards.

The combined number of rushing yards and kickoff return yards (547) for Jim Kerr during the 1960 season. Kerr carried the football 93 times for 389 yards and 8 touchdowns. He also returned 8 kicks for 158 yards.

The number of solo tackles (548) credited to the Penn State defense during the 1998 season. A pair of star linebackers, Brandon Short and LaVar Arrington, led the way with 49 solo stops apiece.

The number of receiving yards (549) amassed by wide receiver Tony Johnson during the 2002 season. Johnson caught 34 passes with three touchdowns, finishing behind another pair of Johnsons (Bryant and Larry) on the receiving yardage list.

The career bowl record for passing yards (550) set by Tony Sacca. The quarterback played in three straight bowl games at the 1989 Holiday Bowl, the 1990 Blockbuster Bowl, and the 1992 Fiesta Bowl. Sacca threw four of his seven postseason touchdown passes in the Fiesta Bowl victory over Tennessee.

The number of wins and year (5, '51) for Penn State in 1951—Rip Engle's second season at the helm. The team finished the season 5-4.

552 The month and year (5, '52) that *The Daily Collegian* reported Penn State would play a 10-game schedule for the 1952 season. The Lions had not played a 10-game season for 21 years prior.

553 The number of rushing yards over the 2,000 yard mark (553) totaled by the Penn State ground game during the 2005 season. Thanks to Larry Johnson's record shattering season and a stout front seven, Penn State more than doubled its opponent's rushing total of 1,116.

554 The number of spectators on hand (554) over 45,000 at the 1993 Blockbuster Bowl between Penn State and Stanford. The bowl game—Penn State's last as an independent before joining the Big Ten—pitted Joe Paterno against legend Bill Walsh.

555 The NFL career completion percentage (55.5) posted by Kerry Collins through the 2007 season. The veteran quarterback learned the professional ropes with the expansion Carolina Panthers. He revitalized his career—and looked a lot like the signal caller who engineered Penn State's prolific offenses in the early 1990s—with the New York Giants. He led the 2000 Giants to the Super Bowl after finishing the regular season with a career best 22 touchdown passes.

556 The winning percentage (.556) of Joe Bedenk in his only season as head coach. The longtime assistant replaced Bob Higgins and finished with a 5-4 record in 1949. He resigned at the end of the season. The student newspaper, *The Daily Collegian*, then began campaigning for a "big-time coach for a big-time college."

557 The total number of offensive yards (557) the Penn State offense racked up per game heading into a Top Ten clash against Michigan during the 1994 season. The Nittany Lion offense did its part with 31 points and 444 total yards, but it was the big play made by the much maligned defense that kept dreams of an undefeated season alive. Brian Miller intercepted Todd Collins' fourth down pass with 1:26 to play to preserve a 7-point victory.

558 The AP ranking of Army and the year (#5, '58) in which PSU played the Cadets at Michie Stadium in West Point, NY and came home with a 26-0 loss. The team finished the season at 6-3-1.

559 The month and year (5, '59) that *The Daily Collegian* reported that the Virginia Military Institute had been added to the PSU schedule for the 1959 fall season. Penn State beat VMI, 21-0, in the second game of the season.

560 The team-best number of rushing yards (560) for Steve Geise during the 1975 season. Geise carried the football 116 times for three touchdowns and 4.8 yards per carry. The running back, as of the 2007 season, sat 25th on Penn State's all-time rushing list with 1,362 yards and 11 touchdowns.

561 The number of yards over the 2,000-yard plateau (561) Penn State's defense allowed through the air in 2006. Anthony Morelli bettered that number with 2,599 yards passing—an average of just under 200 yards per contest.

562 The field goal percentage (56.2) posted by Robbie Gould during the 2003 season. Gould was a perfect 7 for 7 from 20-39 yards, but he struggled from longer distances—2 for 9 from 40 yards and out.

563 The team-best number of rushing yards (563) for Tony Orsini during the 1950 season. Orsini averaged 3.9 yards per carry on 146 attempts with five rushing scores for the Nittany Lions, who won their last four games to salvage a 5-3-1 season.

564 The completion percentage (56.4) of Penn State quarterbacks during the 2002 season. Starter Zack Mills completed 56.5% of his tosses, while back-ups Michael Robinson and Chris Ganter combined for 55.5% in limited duty under center.

565 The number of times (565) Curtis Enis' number was called during his collegiate career. Enis rushed for 3,256 yards and 36 touchdowns from 1995-97.

The AP ranking of Georgia Tech and the year (#5, '66) in which Penn State played the Yellow Jackets at Bobby Dodd Stadium in Atlanta, GA and came home with a 21-0 loss.

The completion percentage (56.7) for Tony Rados in a 20-20 tie against All-American quarterback Dale Samuels and Purdue on September 27, 1952. Rados threw for 179 yards and one touchdown on 17 of 30 passing against the Boilermakers.

The number of penalty yards (568) for Penn State's opponents during the 2002 season. The Nittany Lions were flagged 64 times (two times less than their opponents) for 546 yards.

The winning percentage (.569) for William "Pop" Golden from 1900-02. Golden led the Nittany Lions to a 16-12-1 mark over three seasons before resigning to become the school's first athletic director.

The number of solo tackles (570) credited to the Penn State defense throughout the 2000 season. James Boyd led the way with 84 solo tackles and Justin Kurpeikis recorded 55 solo stops.

The AP ranking and year (#5, '71) that the Lions earned in 1971 after posting an 11-1 record, including a 30-6 victory over Texas in the Cotton Bowl.

The number of receiving yards (572) accumulated by Jack Curry during the 1965 season. Curry caught 42 passes for an average of 13.6 yards per catch and two touchdowns.

The team leading rushing total (573) for Leroy Thompson during the 1990 season. Thompson carried the football 152 times for a 3.8 yard average and eight touchdowns. Thompson's season was sandwiched between the rushing seasons of two Penn State stars (Blair Thomas in 1989 and Richie Anderson in 1991).

The draft round and year (5, '74) in which the Buffalo Bills selected PSU running back Gary Hayman in round five of the 1974 NFL draft as the 106th overall selection. That same year, Heisman award winner John Cappelletti was taken by the Los Angeles Rams as the 11th overall pick in the first round.

575 The number of yards (575) John Bruno, Jr.'s punts traveled over the 2,000-yard mark during the 1985 season. Bruno punted 60 times for an average of 42.9 yards per punt.

576 The number of passing yards (576) Penn State's defense surrendered through the air to Brigham Young's Ty Detmer in the 1989 Holiday Bowl. In their first trip out West since a contest at Stanford in 1973, the Nittany Lions came out victorious behind Blair Thomas and 206 yards passing from Tony Sacca.

577 The number of interception return yards (577) totaled by safety Darren Perry during his NFL career. Perry intercepted 35 passes, with a career best seven coming during the 1994 season for the Pittsburgh Steelers. Perry intercepted 15 passes as a Nittany Lion star through 1991.

578 The completion percentage (57.8) of Penn State's quarterbacks during the 2007 season. Of the two primary quarterbacks, Anthony Morelli started every game under center, while Daryll Clark tossed six completions on just nine attempts for a 66.7 completion percentage.

579 The completion percentage (57.9) for Dallas Cowboys quarterback Roger Staubach during his final season in 1979—the third straight season former Nittany Lion Tom Rafferty protected the quarterback at right guard. The offensive lineman was named a first-team All-American by Football Writers and *Football News* following his 1975 senior season.

580 The number of rushing yards (580) Charlie Pittman gained on the ground during the 1967 season. In the first of his three seasons as a mainstay in the backfield, Pittman averaged 4.9 yards per carry with six touchdowns.

581 The number of kickoff return yards (581) totaled by cornerback A.J. Wallace in the 2007 season. Wallace returned 22 kickoffs for a 26.4-yard average and a touchdown.

582 The completion percentage (58.2) for Anthony Morelli during the 2007 season. The inconsistent Morelli threw for 2,651 yards, with 19 touchdowns, 10 interceptions, and a 124.2 efficiency rating.

583 The combined number of total offensive yards and touchdowns (583) posted by running back Ted Shattuck during the 1951 campaign. He amassed 579 total yards and 4 touchdowns. His number was called 135 times, and he answered the bell with 4.3 yards per carry.

584 The number of receiving yards (584) accumulated by Jack Curry during the 1966 campaign. In the second of a three-season stint as Penn State's main receiver, Curry caught 34 passes with one touchdown.

585 The number of rushing attempts (585) compiled by Penn State's opponents during the 2003 campaign. The Nittany Lions ran just 397 times for 1,747 yards (an average of 3.7 yards per carry).

586 The number of yards (586) Bob Parsons' punts traveled over the 2,000-yard mark during the 1971 season. Parsons booted 41 punts for a 38.7 yard average in the second of his three seasons as the main punter.

587 The draft round and year (5, '87) in which the St. Louis Cardinals selected PSU punter John Bruno in round five of the 1987 NFL draft as the 126th overall selection. Penn State had 13 players selected in the 1987 draft.

588 The number of wins and year (5, '88) in which PSU managed to come out victorious in just five games. The team finished the season with a 21-3 loss in South Bend to #1 ranked Notre Dame and a disappointing 5-6 record.

589 The average number of rushing yards per game (58.9) posted by Lydell Mitchell during his nine-year NFL career with the

Baltimore Colts, the San Diego Chargers, and the Los Angeles Rams. Mitchell eclipsed the 1,000-yard barrier in three consecutive seasons (1975-77) with the Colts, earning Pro Bowl and All-Pro recognition in each campaign.

590 The number of rushing yards (59.0) gained by Rutgers during its October 7, 1989 meeting with Penn State. PSU came away from East Rutherford with a 17-0 win, handing the Scarlet Knights their first loss of the season. The Lions finished the year with an 8-3-1 record and a Holiday Bowl victory.

591 The number of kickoff return yards (591) accumulated by Roger Kochman throughout his collegiate career. Kochman returned 23 kickoffs for a 25.7-yard average, including a 100-yard touchdown return in a 1959 loss to Syracuse.

592 The number of losses and year (5, '92) for PSU in 1992 —a seriously disheartening number, considering the Nittany Lions began the year 5-0. The team finished the season 7-5 and a #24 ranking.

593 The number of ranked opponents and year (5, '93) in which Penn State played five ranked opponents. The Nittany Lions ended the season at 10-2, with both losses coming against Top 25 teams.

594 The career touchdown pass percentage (5.94) posted by Kerry Collins while wearing the blue and white. Collins wasn't just a leader with his arm, but with his actions off the field. He donated $250,000 to the University for a Scholarship to be given to quarterback recruits.

595 The career NFL completion percentage (59.5) for Chuck Fusina. The successful college quarterback never saw his career materialize at the next level, where he played just four seasons between the Tampa Bay Buccaneers and the Green Bay Packers without a single start. Fusina threw for only 198 yards and one touchdown with the Buccaneers during the 1981 campaign.

596   The number of penalty yards (596) called against Penn State's opponents in 2007. The Nittany Lions were flagged 10 times less (58) for a total of 446 yards.

597   The number of ranked opponents and year (5, '97) in which Penn State played five ranked opponents. The Nittany Lions ended the season 9-3 going 3-2 against Top 25 teams.

598   The overall pick and the year (5, '98) in which PSU running back Curtis Enis was selected by the Chicago Bears with the fifth overall pick in the 1998 NFL draft. Enis went on to score four touchdowns and tally 1,497 rushing yards during his professional career.

599   The number of yards (599) Jamie Dresse's punts traveled over the 1,000-yard plateau during the 1992 season. Dresse booted 39 punts for a 41-yard average in his lone season as the punter in Happy Valley.

600   The team-best number of receiving yards (600) Mickey Shuler posted as a tight end in 1977. Shuler caught 33 passes with one touchdown, just one season after he led the team with 21 catches for 281 yards and three touchdowns.

Todd Blackledge, NFL Stats (1983-89)

Year	Team	Games	Starts	CMP	ATT	CMP%	YDS	TD	INT	RAT
1983	Kansas City	4	0	20	34	58.8	259	3	0	112.3
1984	Kansas City	11	8	147	294	50.0	1,707	6	11	59.2
1985	Kansas City	12	6	86	172	50.0	1,190	6	14	50.3
1986	Kansas City	10	8	96	211	45.5	1,200	10	6	67.6
1987	Kansas City	3	2	15	31	48.4	154	1	1	60.4
1988	Pittsburgh	3	3	38	79	48.1	494	2	3	60.8
1989	Pittsburgh	3	2	22	60	36.7	282	1	3	36.9
Career		**46**	**29**	**424**	**881**	**48.1**	**5,286**	**29**	**38**	**60.2**

"I can tell you that virtually all of the players he's touched in fifty years as an assistant and head coach have been enriched by the experience. I consider myself and I know my teammates and Penn State players past and present feel likewise, a better person for having played for Joe Paterno."

—*Todd Blackledge in the foreword to the book Quotable Joe*

Chapter Seven

The College Todd Blackledge

In the real world, an individual takes what he or she learns in college and becomes successful in a field of choice later down the road.

For Todd Blackledge, it appeared the reverse was true. Everything he accomplished while grooming his right arm for years of fame and fortune in the NFL matters inside Penn State's pearly gates. Outside, especially in the pigskin proud Midwestern city of Kansas City, his decorated collegiate days are a footnote in a brief and disappointing professional career.

Blackledge was part of a quarterback class that included three legendary signal callers: John Elway, Dan Marino, and Jim Kelly. The Kansas City Chiefs made him their first-round draft choice and banked a boatload of success on his golden right arm.

The pedigree never correlated into performance. The reasons are forever unclear and truly aren't important when assessing the quarterback who led Penn State to the 1982 national championship.

Born within the city limits of the Pro Football Hall of Fame in Canton, Ohio, Blackledge appeared destined for great things. He was a winner, leading the Nittany Lions to Joe Paterno's first national championship and compiling a 31-5 record as a starter. He was a talented passer, throwing for 4,812 yards and 41 touchdowns from 1980-82, and setting the single season touchdown pass mark with 22 scoring tosses in 1982.

He was also a risk-taker, a riverboat gambler with the confidence and rocket arm to make throws into tight spaces. The success was as frequent (358 yards and two touchdowns against the Miami Hurricanes in 1981) as the failure (the dubious record for most career interceptions at 41).

He never even made honorable mention All-American, yet was rewarded with the Davey O'Brien Award as the nation's top quarterback following the 1982 season. That distinction, coupled with a championship ring, made him a valued commodity at the next level, and earned him lifetime appreciation at Penn State.

Blackledge spent five seasons with the Chiefs and two more with the Pittsburgh Steelers before retiring from the league. He threw 29 touchdowns to 38 interceptions, and started just 29 games in seven seasons.

It was a far cry from what he accomplished as a Nittany Lion. He threw four touchdown passes in a game three times during the 1982 season, and threw more passes (292) than any quarterback since Chuck Fusina (246) in 1977. He tossed a touchdown pass and threw for 228 yards in the championship clinching Sugar Bowl victory over Georgia.

He spent much of his off field time working on his studies. He earned a Bachelor of Arts degree in Speech Communication, graduating Phi Beta Kappa with a 3.8 grade point average. He was a first team Academic All-American and earned the Eric Walker Award given annually to the senior student who best enhances the esteem and recognition of the university.

Blackledge worked as a radio host in Cleveland and Canton and became a college football analyst for ABC Sports in 1994. He moved on to CBS Sports as the lead college football analyst in 1999, and took his speaking skills and knowledge of the game to ESPN as the lead primetime college football analyst in 2006. He was inducted into the Academic All-America Hall of Fame in 1997 and now sits on the Board of Visitors for Penn State's Center for Sports Journalism.

It reads like a very successful career and a lesson for college football players everywhere. Todd Blackledge became successful later in life because of what he learned at Penn State.

In the classroom.

The number of rushing yards (601) Lenny Moore accumulated on the ground during the 1953 campaign. Moore went on to a Hall of Fame career with the Baltimore Colts, finishing with 113 total touchdowns and 7 Pro Bowl selections. He was inducted into the Pro Football Hall of Fame in 1975.

The team leading number of rushing yards (602) gained by Fran Rogel during the 1948 season. Rogel led the Nittany Lions in rushing for three consecutive campaigns, compiling 499 yards in 1947, and 395 yards in 1949.

The number of all-purpose yards (60.3) Kenny Watson averaged per contest in the 1999 campaign. The Harrisburg, PA native accumulated 522 kickoff return yards, 97 punt return yards, 38 receiving yards, and 67 rushing yards to total 724 all-purpose yards for the year.

The career high completion percentage (60.4) posted by Milt Plum during his 1960 All-Pro campaign with the Cleveland Browns. Plum threw 21 touchdown passes to just five interceptions in the best of his 13-year professional career. The former PSU signal caller also served as a punter during his collegiate days, and he boomed a 73-and 56-yard punts in a 7-6 upset victory over Ohio State in 1956.

The number of all-purpose yards (605) compiled by Bill Luther during the 1949 season. Luther racked up 405 return yards to go along with 200 rushing yards as Fran Rogel's backup.

The number of passes (606) completed by Zack Mills throughout his Penn State career. Mills entered the starting lineup during his freshman year and ended up with more passing yards than any other quarterback in Penn State history (7,212). Mills also set career records for attempts (1,082) and completions (606), while throwing 41 touchdowns and 39 interceptions.

The winning percentage (.607) of Bob Higgins from 1930-48. The assistant coach was promoted to the top job after Hugo Bezdek was relieved of his head coaching duties and named director of the School of Physical Education.

Penn State's conference winning percentage (.608) from its first Big Ten season in 1993 through the 2007 campaign. The Nittany Lions won at least a share of two conference titles during that time, including their memorable Run to the Roses with an 8-0 mark in 1994.

The number of career kickoff return yards (609) Shelly Hammonds racked up from 1990-93. Hammonds handled 23 kickoffs for an average of 24.4 yards per return. Hammonds may be best known for his shining moment in the Penn State backfield during the 1990 season. The redshirt freshman and former safety ran for 208 yards and a pair of lengthy touchdowns in a 40-21 victory over Boston College.

The number of home games and the year (6, '10) for Penn State during the 1910 season. Penn State's home record that year was 5-0-1 under Coach Jack Hollenback.

The number of shutouts and the year (6, '11) Penn State blanked its opponents six times. The Nittany Lions closed out the season 8-0-1 overall, after outscoring their opponents 190-15.

The number of career punt return yards (612) piled up by Rich Mauti during his NFL career from 1977-84. Mauti also served as a kickoff return specialist and wide receiver for the New Orleans Saints and the Washington Redskins, and he made the All-Pro team in 1980 after accumulating 798 kick return yards and 111 punt return yards with the Saints. Mauti served a similar role as a Nittany Lion and caught a 21-yard pass from Chuck Fusina in the 1976 Gator Bowl.

The number of receiving yards (613) accumulated by D.J. Dozier during his collegiate career. Dozier ran for 3,227 yards and added 55 return yards for 3,895 all-purpose yards from 1983-86.

The number of receiving yards (614) posted by 33-year-old Joe Jurevicius during his 2007 campaign with the Cleveland Browns. The veteran caught 50 passes with three touchdowns and played in all 16 games. Jurevicius has carved out a solid professional career after an impressive collegiate resume built at Penn State. He led the team with 41 catches for 869 yards and four touchdowns during his junior season.

The number of games ending in shutouts and the year (6, '15) for Penn State in 1915. The Lions posted an overall 7-2 record for Coach Dick Harlow after posting shutouts against Westminster (26-0), Lebanon Valley (13-0), West Virginia Wesleyan (28-0), and Lehigh (7-0), but the club also suffered two shutouts, losing at Harvard (0-13) and at Pittsburgh (0-20).

The number of rushing yards (616) racked up by Lydell Mitchell during the 1969 season. In a precursor to his incredible 1971 campaign, Mitchell averaged 5.5 yards per carry with six touchdowns.

The number of rushing attempts (617) for Penn State during the 1970 season. The Nittany Lions totaled 2,769 rushing yards with 31 touchdowns. Lydell Mitchell and Franco Harris led the prolific ground game.

The total number of offensive yards (618) over the 2,000-yard mark posted by Zack Mills during the 2002 season. Mills threw for 2,417 yards, but also showcased his shifty running style with 201 yards on the ground.

The total number of offensive yards (619) for fullback Sean McHugh during his four years as a Nittany Lion. McHugh helped pave the way into the record book for Larry Johnson in 2002, and ran for 322 yards and six touchdowns of his own from 2000-03. McHugh also caught 44 passes for 297 yards and one touchdown. He was taken by the Tennessee Titans in the seventh round of the 2004 NFL draft.

620 The number of rushing yards (620) Blair Thomas gained during his rookie season with the New York Jets in 1990. Thomas averaged a career best 5.0 yards per carry and caught 20 passes for 204 yards.

621 The team leading number of rushing yards (621) compiled by Woody Petchel during the 1975 season. Petchel carried the football 148 times with 5 touchdowns, and averaged 4.2 yards per carry.

622 The team rushing yards record in a single game (622) attained in a 1924 contest against Lebanon Valley. The Nittany Lions used the rushing attack to ground Lebanon Valley, 47-3.

623 The career touchdown pass percentage (6.23) tallied by Todd Blackledge from 1980-82. The Canton, Ohio native never finished higher than honorable mention All-American, but he was the second Penn State player inducted into the GTE/CoSIDA Academic Hall of Fame.

624 The number of college football purists (624) over 16,000 that braved the elements on a cold, windy day at the 1960 Liberty Bowl in Philadelphia. Penn State's loyal followers were not disappointed, as the Nittany Lion defense caused four turnovers in a 41-12 rout of Oregon.

625 The team-leading number of rushing yards (625) compiled by Tom Urbanik during the 1964 campaign. Urbanik averaged 4.7 yards per carry and scored eight touchdowns for Penn State, which rebounded from a 1-4 start to complete a 6-4 season that included a 27-0 waxing of #2 Ohio State.

626 The number of games ending in shutouts and the year (6, '26) for PSU in 1926. The Lions posted an overall 5-4 record for Coach Hugo Bezdek after posting shutouts against Susquehanna (82-0), Lebanon Valley (35-0), and Bucknell (9-0), but the club also suffered three shutouts, losing at Notre Dame (0-28), against Syracuse (0-10) during Homecoming, and at Pennsylvania (0-3).

The number of wins and the year (6, '27) for PSU during the 1927 season for an overall 6-2-2 record. PSU was 4-2 at New Beaver Field in State College.

The number of yards (628) Elwood Petchel threw for during the 1948 season. Petchel completed 48 of 100 passes with nine touchdowns, but he also returned 14 punts for 144 yards and intercepted four passes on defense.

The number of consecutive unblocked punts (629) before Pitt blocked Ralph Giacomarro's punt in a 29-14 loss to the Panthers on December 1, 1979.

The number of receiving yards (630) Scott Fitzkee accounted for during the 1978 campaign. Fitzkee caught 37 passes with six touchdowns on the season, and finished his career with 65 receptions for 1,263 yards and 11 scores.

The number of career NFL receiving yards (631) for running back Gary Brown. The bruising running back rushed for over 1,000 yards twice during his eight-year career, and finished with 4,300 yards rushing for the Houston Oilers, the New York Giants, and the San Diego Chargers. Brown was a solid contributor in the Penn State backfield during the late 1980s through 1990.

The number of total offensive yards (632) Penn State racked up in a 66-14 victory over Texas Christian in 1971. That number was one of the highest in school history (keep reading for the highest offensive output!).

The number of team leading receiving yards (633) Deon Butler accumulated during the 2007 season. Butler caught 47 passes with four touchdowns as part of a wide receiver rotation that included Derrick Williams, Jordan Norwood, Terrell Golden, and Chris Bell.

634 The completion percentage (63.4) of Penn State's opposing quarterbacks during the 2002 season. The PSU defense did rise to the occasion with 20 interceptions—four each from safety Shawn Mayer and shutdown cornerback Bryan Scott.

635 The number of points scored and the year (6, '35) in which Lebanon Valley scored six points in Penn State's 1935 season opener. The Nittany Lions won the game 12-6, but after winning the first three contests of the season, Coach Bob Higgins guided the club to a disappointing 4-4 overall record after dropping four of its final five games.

636 The number of pages (636) in Ridge Riley's historical look at Penn State football titled *Road to Number One: A Personal Chronicle of Penn State Football*. The book was released in 1977 with head coach Joe Paterno—obviously not Mike Poorman—penning the foreword.

637 The number of receiving yards (637) racked up by Deon Butler during the 2006 campaign. Butler was a speed demon on the field and a reliable presence on the stat sheet for the Nittany Lions, posting his second straight season of 600-plus yards receiving. He caught 48 passes for a 13.3-yard average and two touchdowns.

638 The number of rushing yards (638) for fullback Matt Suhey during the 1977 season. Suhey was a valuable piece of Penn State's offensive puzzle during each of his four seasons in Happy Valley. The fullback trap and dive plays were called often, and Suhey answered the bell with 4.6 yards per carry and 8 scores.

639 The number of points and the year (6, '39) in which Penn State scored just six points in its 1939 game against Syracuse. Luckily, the defense held the Orangemen to only six points as well, and the contest on October 28 at Archbold Stadium in Syracuse resulted in a 6-6 draw. The Lions closed out the 1939 season 5-1-2 overall.

640 The team leading number of passing yards (640) for Vince O'Bara during the 1950 season. O'Bara completed just 38 of 103 passes, but three of those went for touchdowns.

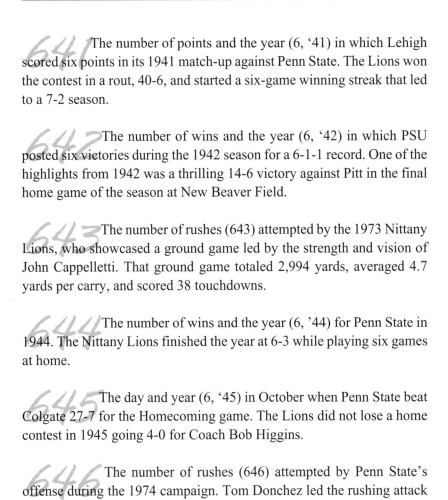

The number of points and the year (6, '41) in which Lehigh scored six points in its 1941 match-up against Penn State. The Lions won the contest in a rout, 40-6, and started a six-game winning streak that led to a 7-2 season.

The number of wins and the year (6, '42) in which PSU posted six victories during the 1942 season for a 6-1-1 record. One of the highlights from 1942 was a thrilling 14-6 victory against Pitt in the final home game of the season at New Beaver Field.

The number of rushes (643) attempted by the 1973 Nittany Lions, who showcased a ground game led by the strength and vision of John Cappelletti. That ground game totaled 2,994 yards, averaged 4.7 yards per carry, and scored 38 touchdowns.

The number of wins and the year (6, '44) for Penn State in 1944. The Nittany Lions finished the year at 6-3 while playing six games at home.

The day and year (6, '45) in October when Penn State beat Colgate 27-7 for the Homecoming game. The Lions did not lose a home contest in 1945 going 4-0 for Coach Bob Higgins.

The number of rushes (646) attempted by Penn State's offense during the 1974 campaign. Tom Donchez led the rushing attack in the first season of the post-John Cappelletti era.

The number of shutouts and the year (6, '47) in which PSU blanked six of its opponents and finished the 1947 season with a 9-0-1 record for Coach Bob Higgins. Its only blemish was a 13-13 tie against #4 Southern Methodist University at the Cotton Bowl—the last game of the season.

The career touchdown passing percentage (6.48) registered by John Sacca from 1992-93. Sacca started for the Nittany Lions during the 1992 season but quit the team and left school after the third game during the 1993 campaign.

The number of carries (649) for Curt Warner during his record-setting collegiate career. Warner is best remembered for his school record 3,398 rushing yards and a steady dose of end zone visits (24 career rushing scores).

The number of rushing yards (65.0) gained by running back Evan Royster in the 2007 Alamo Bowl against Texas A&M. PSU won the game 24-17 in Joe Pa's 500th game. Royster also scored on a 38-yard scamper in the fourth quarter to help the Lions end the season with a 9-4 mark.

The number of total offensive yards (651) the Penn State defense yielded to Brigham Young's clockwork offense in the 1989 Holiday Bowl. The Cougars efficient offense was spectacular on the stat sheet, but on the scoreboard Penn State prevailed 50-39, due in part to Leroy Thompson's 68 yards rushing and two touchdowns.

The number of receiving yards (652) collected by wide receiver Eddie Drummond during the 1999 season. Drummond caught a career best 35 passes for 652 yards and five touchdowns.

The number of wins and the year (6, '53) in which PSU posted six victories to finish the season with a 6-3 record. One of the highlights of the season was a 17-0 victory on November 21 against in-state rival Pitt.

The number of times (654) Tony Hunt's number was called during his workmanlike collegiate career. Hunt sported plenty of bumps and bruises in a four-year run through the record book that ended with 3,320 career rushing yards, the most rushing attempts in program history, and heaps of praise from coaches, players, and loyal Lion fans.

The combined number of career NFL punt return and kickoff return yards (655) amassed by Bob Campbell. He piled up 133 punt return yards and 522 kick return yards. The multipurpose threat starred at Penn State as a running back, receiver, and return specialist, but he played just one season in the NFL with Pittsburgh after the Steelers selected him in the fourth round of the 1969 NFL draft.

656 The number of all-purpose yards (656) Larry Joe totaled during the 1947 season. The special teams ace racked up 306 return yards to go along with 350 rushing yards for the Nittany Lions, who ran through the regular season unblemished before tying Southern Methodist in the Cotton Bowl to finish with a 9-0-1 record.

657 The number of passes (657) attempted by Kerry Collins during his collegiate career. Despite piling up record after record during the 1994 campaign, Collins still didn't attempt as many collegiate passes as his predecessor, Tony Sacca.

658 The number of passes (658) attempted by Todd Blackledge during his decorated collegiate career. Blackledge completed 341 passes for 4,812 yards and a school record 41 touchdowns to go along with a school record 41 interceptions. Tony Sacca and Zack Mills later tied Blackledge's touchdown mark.

659 The combined number of career punt return yards (659) racked up by Ron Younker (281) and Lenny Moore (378). The duo's successful special teams work helped win plenty of games in Happy Valley, as Younker returned punts in 1953 and 1954, and Moore pulled duty from 1953-55.

660 The number of receiving yards (660) racked up by Nick Sukay during his senior season at Greensburg Central Catholic. Sukay committed to Penn State as an early enrollee following his 2006 senior season and redshirted his freshman year at PSU in 2007.

661 The number of total offensive yards (661) Penn State accumulated during a 1995 rout of Rutgers, 59-34. Controversy followed the meeting between a pair of state universities. Reserve quarterback Mike McQueary threw a 42-yard touchdown pass to Chris Campbell with 58 seconds left, leaving Rutgers head coach Doug Graber steamed at the late score. Joe Paterno agreed after the game, saying, "Doug was upset and has a right to be. I didn't intend to do that."

662 The number of receiving yards (662) Curt Warner amassed over the course of his collegiate career. Warner also totaled 922 return yards to go along with his record rushing mark, for 4,982 career all-purpose yards.

663 The number of times and the year (6, '63) in which PSU failed to score 20 or more points in a game, but still managed to finish the season with a winning record of 7-3 overall. In those 10 games, neither the Lions nor their opponents scored 30 points or more.

664 The number of wins and the year (6, '64) in which PSU posted six victories to end the season at 7-4. The Nittany Lions started 1964 by going 1-4, but were able to turn things around and won five straight to close out the season.

665 The number of passes (665) attempted by Chuck Fusina from 1975-78. The Pittsburgh, PA native ended his collegiate career with the most first place votes for the 1978 Heisman Trophy. However, for just the second time in Heisman history, the winner (Oklahoma running back Billy Simms) had fewer first place votes but a larger second and third place margin, thus claiming the trophy.

666 The number of rushing yards (666) accumulated by Roger Kochman during the 1961 campaign. Kochman's number was called 129 times with six touchdowns. After missing the entire 1960 season following a preseason knee injury, Kochman changed his rushing style from straight ahead speed to shifty cutbacks with great results. He added 226 yards receiving and another three scores.

667 The school record completion percentage (66.7) for quarterback Kerry Collins during the undefeated 1994 campaign. The strong-armed signal caller also set single season school records for total offense (2,660), completions (176), passing yards (2,679), and passing efficiency (172.86).

668 The number of all-purpose yards (668) totaled by wide receiver Derrick Williams during his first season in Happy Valley. As the nation's top prep player, Williams rushed for 105 yards, sprinted for 274 kick return yards, and piled up 289 receiving yards in his first season as a

Nittany Lion. He missed the final five games of the season after breaking his arm in the Michigan game.

The number of rushing yards (669) Tony Hunt posted six games into the 2006 season. Hunt was coming off a 144-yard workhorse performance in a 28-27 overtime victory over Minnesota when the Nittany Lions hosted Michigan. The unbeaten Wolverines held the power runner to 33 yards—78 below his season average—on just 13 carries in a 17-10 victory at Beaver Stadium.

The number of rushing yards (670) accumulated by QB Rashard Casey during his time at Penn State. Casey normally used his elusive instincts to evade rushers and find open receivers, but on occasion he broke free and scrambled for valuable yardage.

The number of career punt return yards (671) totaled by Kevin Baugh from 1980-83. Baugh's best special teams work came during the 1982 campaign, when he returned 29 punts for 315 yards (10.8 yards per return average).

The number of rushing yards (67.2) Michael Robinson averaged per contest during the 2005 season. Robinson was named the Big Ten's Offensive Player of the Year by the coaches, and was a consensus second-team All-Big Ten selection after racking up a single season school record 3,156 yards of total offense.

The number of passing yards (673) piled up by Al Jacks during the 1957 season. Jacks completed 53 of 103 passes with five touchdowns and three interceptions for Penn State, which won four of its last five games to cap off a 6-3 season.

The number of points and the year (6, '74) in which Navy held Penn State to only six points and claimed a 7-6 triumph at Beaver Stadium on September 21, 1974. It was the Lions' first loss of the season en route to 10-2 record for the year.

The number of points (675) Penn State received in the final 2002 AP poll. The Nittany Lions (9-4) finished the season one spot below upstart Boise State and one spot above perennial power Notre Dame in 16th position.

The career bowl winning percentage (.676) of Joe Paterno through the 2007 Alamo Bowl. The 24-17 victory over Texas A&M was Paterno's all-time record 23rd bowl victory in 34 chances.

The number of weeks and the year (6, '77) in which Penn State spent six weeks ranked among the Top 25. The Lions held a #20 ranking before losing 20-9 at the hands of #15 Notre Dame in the Gator Bowl.

The number of kickoff return yards (678) racked up by the Penn State special teams during the 2006 season. The Nittany Lions averaged 21.2 yards per return with A.J. Wallace and Rodney Kinlaw seeing the majority of action.

The winning percentage (.679) of Rip Engle during his 16 seasons as head coach. The former Brown head coach turned down head coaching opportunities at Yale, Wisconsin, and Pittsburgh before heading for Penn State.

The total number of offensive yards (680) accumulated by Dick Hoak during the 1960 season. Hoak was a part of 112 offensive plays for the Nittany Lions, who won their last five games of the season to finish with a respectable 7-3 mark.

The number of career receiving yards (681) credited to Larry Johnson—part of his career all-purpose yard record of 5,045 yards. Johnson ran for 2,933 yards and gained 1,411 yards in the return game from 1999-2002.

The strength of schedule percentage (.682) for the 1996 Nittany Lions, who posted an 11-2 record with losses to Iowa and Ohio State. Penn State defeated Southern California, Louisville, Wisconsin, and Michigan in the regular season before trouncing Texas in the Fiesta Bowl.

The number of rushing yards (683) Curtis Enis gained on 113 carries during the 1995 season. Enis displayed flashes of stardom during his freshman campaign, averaging an eye-popping 6.0 yards per carry and scoring four touchdowns.

PSU posted six victories during the 1984 season (6, '84)—but they should have done better. The Nittany Lions closed out the season with a 6-5 record after losing three of their last four contests.

The number of home games and the year (6, '85) in which PSU went a perfect 6-0 at home en route to an 11-1 season. The Lions suffered a heartbreaking 25-10 loss to Oklahoma in the 1986 Orange Bowl.

The school record for passing yards (686) in consecutive games set by Zack Mills during the 2002 season. One week after torching the Iowa secondary for 399 yards, Mills went back to work against the Wisconsin pass defense with 287 yards through the air.

The number of combined points scored (687) by Penn State and Michigan State in their first 10 Big Ten meetings. The Nittany Lions won eight of those first 10 match-ups.

The winning percentage (.688) of Jack Hollenback during his lone season as head coach in 1910. Hollenback led the Nittany Lions to a 5-2-1 mark in place of his younger brother Bill, who resigned to accept a one-year position as head coach at Missouri.

The team leading number of rushing yards (689) piled up by Gary Brown during the 1988 season. The season appeared a lost cause with Blair Thomas sidelined due to a knee injury that kept him out for the entire campaign. Brown did his best to pick up the slack for the Nittany Lions (5-6), but the club still finished with its first losing season since 1938.

The day and year (6, '90) in October when Penn State played Temple as part of the school's Homecoming festivities. The Lions won the game 48-10 at Beaver Stadium. Penn State finished the 1990 season at 9-3.

691 The number of team leading receiving yards (691) posted by Deon Butler during the 2005 season. The Woodbridge, VA native caught a team best 37 passes and scored half (9) of the team's receiving touchdowns.

692 The number of pass attempts (692) by Wally Richardson as Penn State's quarterback in 1992 and 1994-96. Richardson completed 378 passes for 4,419 yards, 27 touchdowns, and 14 interceptions. The signal caller also holds the single game program record for most completions (33) in a 17-9 loss to Wisconsin in 1995.

693 The number of career victories (693) from Penn State women's basketball coach Rene Portland before she resigned in 2007. The significance to Penn State pigskin, you ask? Portland was hired by Joe Paterno when he served as the university's athletic director. Paterno worked as athletic director from 1980-82.

694 The number of rushing yards (694) running back Mike Archie gained over the 1,000-yard plateau as a Nittany Lion from 1992-95. Archie's number was called 305 times for 1,694 yards and 14 rushing touchdowns. Ki-Jana Carter's blocking and change of pace back was selected by the Houston Oilers in the seventh-round of the 1996 NFL draft.

695 The AP ranking and the year (#6, '95) when #6 Penn State played Wisconsin. The Badgers handed PSU its first loss of the season, 17-9. The Lions went on to finish the season at 9-3 overall and 5-3 in Big Ten action.

696 The field goal percentage (69.6) for left-footer Kevin Kelly over the course of the 2005 season. Kelly connected on 16 of 23 field goals and 49 of 50 extra points for a team best 99 points, 33 more than the second highest total amassed by Michael Robinson.

697 The number of receiving yards (697) Kenny Jackson racked up to become Penn State's first All-American wide receiver in 1982. He caught 41 passes and reached the end zone seven times during that national championship season. By the time his collegiate career ended one year later, Jackson owned 27 school records and again received All-American recognition.

698 The number of points and the year (6, '98) in which Penn State held Southern Miss to only six points during the 1998 season opener. The Nittany Lions won the contest 34-6 in front of 96,617 screaming fans, and went on to post a 9-3 overall record on the season.

699 The AP ranking and the year (#6, '99) when #6 Penn State met the Michigan Wolverines in 1999. ABC aired the contest as Michigan beat PSU 31-27 in front of 96,840 fans.

700 The number of program wins (700) compiled by Penn State with a 23-20 victory over Wisconsin in Madison on September 28, 1996. Penn State became just the sixth school to reach 700 victories.

Michael Robinson, Penn State Stats (2002-05)

Season	Games	CMP	ATT	CMP%	YDS	TD	INT	Rush	Yards	AVG	TD
2002	13	10	17	58.8	119	0	1	50	263	5.3	6
2003	11	62	138	44.9	892	5	5	107	396	3.7	3
2004	4	5	8	62.5	87	1	0	22	99	4.5	0
2005	12	162	311	52.1	2,350	17	10	163	806	4.9	11
Total	**40**	**239**	**474**	**50.4**	**3,448**	**23**	**16**	**342**	**1,564**	**4.57**	**20**

> "When the world says 'Give Up,' hope whispers
> 'Try it one more time.'"
>
> *—Anonymous*

Chapter Eight

Michael, God, and the Penn State Pigskin

*F*aith is based in it. Its strength is not always self evident in sight, but it is powerful to the soul.

Prayer.

It is what kept Michael Robinson grounded. It is what kept his determination high during days spent far away from under center. It is what kept him humble during a senior season normally written far west in Hollywood.

And frankly, it is what kept him in Happy Valley.

In Robinson's mind, he woke up every morning to cloudy skies. He never saw the blue and the white, the sun that shined just above the crest of Mount Nittany.

No matter what he did on the field—and he was moderately successful as both a runner and receiver—Robinson was dubbed a miscast athlete without a true home. He sat behind Zack Mills at his dream position, losing out to a southpaw with nary a zip on his passes or a visible muscle on his skinny frame.

Robinson was the jacked poster boy with the Superman tattoo and a personality that sparkled with each engaging smile. Mills was the stable presence, the steady hand guiding a patchwork ship.

They were teammates, not enemies. Yet, Mills still stood between Robinson and the quarterback position, regulating the superstar athlete to the slot, the backfield, and special teams duty.

It wasn't what Robinson committed to when he signed the dotted line. He spent nights in his dorm room with a handful of business cards, flipping through different universities and coaches like a fortune teller waiting for a sign.

In time, the skies slowly opened. The clouds didn't dissipate overnight; the doubts didn't disappear in a day, a week, or a month. Just something in Robinson's gut told him Penn State was the place, icon Joe Paterno was the coach, and his chance was on the horizon.

He even discussed the benefits of playing multiple offensive positions. It gave him differing perspectives and forced him to understand the many intricacies of Penn State's basic and more complex packages.

And after three seasons of struggle, success came as a byproduct of faith. He didn't believe it was possible, he knew it was. Such confidence was a part of Robinson's personality and it made him a natural leader on and off the field.

Players almost appointed him captain as a freshman, a rare occurrence in collegiate athletics and an even more unimaginable distinction in Paterno's hierarchal structure. He was selected as one of three captains as a senior in 2005, and he led with his overall ability and his game changing skills in crunch time.

Robinson became the only Nittany Lion quarterback to surpass 1,000 yards rushing and the fifth to reach the 5,000-yard plateau in total offense. He set a single season school record with 3,156 total yards, blowing past Kerry Collins' previous mark of 2,660 yards set in 1994—the year Penn State won its only Big Ten title.

That was before Robinson guided the Nittany Lions to a share of the regular season conference crown and a trip to the 2006 Orange Bowl. He was the coaches' choice for Big Ten Offensive Player of the Year and was a unanimous second-team all-conference selection. He also finished fifth in Heisman Trophy voting, an accomplishment that signified his place in the game, a far cry from his days as a slot receiver and third-down running back.

But Robinson's greatest success occurred when the team needed him most. He led a last minute drive capped by a game-winning touchdown pass to Derrick Williams at Northwestern, and made clutch play after clutch play in a go-ahead scoring drive against Michigan—a game that resulted in a narrow loss and kept Penn State from a perfect season.

That late game success came back to his belief in God.

"Sometimes, I feel like he speaks to me, honestly," Robinson told the *New York Times* during his senior campaign. It was a feeling deeply rooted in his upbringing at the Rising Mount Zion Baptist Church in Richmond, VA.

It was there that Robinson began a journey that took him to the depths of the valley, only to see him rise again at the pinnacle of the mountain.

It sounds like a story written in scripture. And Michael Robinson wouldn't want it any other way.

The number of total offensive yards (701) compiled by quarterback Rich Lucas during the 1958 season. Lucas threw for 483 yards with three touchdowns, and ran for another 218 yards and six scores. The media dubbed him "Riverboat Richie" because of his daring, high-risk play on the field.

The number of receiving yards (702) over the 1,000-yard mark totaled by Tony Johnson from 2000-03. The State College High School product is the son of assistant coach Larry Johnson, Sr.

The U.S. House Resolution (703) that commemorated Penn State University's 150th anniversary. U.S. congressman Mike Doyle spoke about the resolution on July 6, 2004, and stated, "I might add that it also has one hell of a football team, which has been led to many victories over the years by its legendary head coach, Joe Paterno."

704 The number of times and the year (7, '04) in which Penn State held its opponents to fewer than 10 points in a contest. That happened seven times during the 1904 season, and the Nittany Lions won six of those seven games. However, PSU was just 1-3 when giving up double digits during a 6-4 season for head coach Tom Fennell.

705 The number of career receiving yards (705) posted by Jimmy Scott from 1971-73. Scott holds the program record for career receiving yards average after catching 23 passes for 6 touchdowns and a 30.7 yards-per-catch average. The Carlisle, PA native caught a 76-yard pass from John Hufnagel that helped ice a 45-26 rout of Boston College during the 1972 season.

706 The number of rushing yards (706) amassed by Charlie Pittman during his 1969 senior season. The All-American running back averaged 4.7 yards per carry and scored 10 touchdowns on the ground for the Nittany Lions. Charles' son, Charles Anthony "Tony" Pittman, starred as a defensive back on the unbeaten 1994 squad.

707 The total number of receiving yards (707) racked up in Kenny Jackson's six 100-yard receiving games during his career. Jackson caught five passes for a career best 158 yards and two scores at Pittsburgh during the 1981 season, and then caught four balls for 104 yards and two touchdowns in Chestnut Hill against Boston College one year later. He added two other big receiving days during the 1982 season before accumulating 101 receiving yards on seven catches with two touchdowns against Notre Dame, and 108 yards on four catches with two more scores against Pittsburgh as a senior.

708 The number of dancers (708), according to the *Harrisburg Patriot-News,* who didn't sit or sleep during the 46-hour dance marathon at the Bryce Jordan Center in 2008. Penn State football, and Nittany Lion athletics in general, support THON, the largest student run philanthropy in the world. A new record—just over $6.6 million—was set in 2008.

709 The number of penalty yards (709) Penn State's opponents racked up during the 2005 season. By comparison, the Nittany Lions played disciplined, infraction free football with only 422 penalty yards.

710 The number of all-purpose yards (710) Jim Kerr racked up during the 1959 campaign. Kerr racked up 122 receiving yards and 268 return yards to go along with his team best rushing total. He made one of the biggest plays of the season in the third quarter of a 19-8 victory at Missouri, taking a short pass from Rich Lucas 59 yards for a touchdown to break open a tight contest.

711 The school record for total number of offensive yards (711) gained against Susquehanna in 1926. The Nittany Lions came within five yards of that record in an 81-0 triumph over Cincinnati in 1991.

712 The combined number of victories (712) for Joe Paterno and Florida State head coach Bobby Bowden prior to their clash in the 2006 Orange Bowl. The game marked the third bowl meeting between the two proud programs (1967 Gator Bowl, 1990 Blockbuster Bowl), and the Nittany Lions escaped with a thrilling 26-23 triple overtime win.

713 The number of times and the year (7, '13) in which Penn State was held below 20 points during the 1913 season. After beginning the season with back-to-back victories, the Nittany Lions suffered six consecutive defeats to close out the season a miserable 2-6.

714 Dick Harlow's winning percentage (.714) during his three seasons at the helm from 1915-17. Harlow was a multi-sport star during his collegiate career at Penn State, earning two football letters while participating in baseball and track. Harlow also had a successful coaching career outside Happy Valley, earning Coach of the Year honors in 1936 and winning the Ivy League Coach of the Year Award one year later while at Harvard. The Nittany Lion alum was inducted into the National Football Foundation College Football Hall of Fame in 1954.

715 The approximate number of miles (71.5) between Penn State's campus in University Park, PA and Lewisburg, PA. Penn State played and won its first official game against Bucknell in Lewisburg, 54-0, back in 1887.

716 The total number of offensive yards (716) over the 3,000-yard mark totaled by Rashard Casey from 1997-2000. The Hoboken, NJ native threw for 3,046 yards with 302 of them coming in a heartbreaking 26-23 double overtime loss to Iowa during the 2000 season.

717 The career touchdown passing percentage (7.17) recorded by Mike McQueary from 1994-97. The signal caller dubbed "Big Red" for his strawberry locks threw 17 touchdown passes during his best season as a senior.

718 The combined number of receptions and rushing attempts (718) for Richie Anderson during his 12-year NFL career with the New York Jets and the Dallas Cowboys. Anderson racked up 3,149 yards and 14 touchdowns on 400 receptions, and 1,274 yards and four scores on 318 rushes.

719 The number of football loyalists (719) over the 70,000 spectator mark that witnessed Penn State's improbable comeback victory over Kansas in the 1969 Orange Bowl. Penn State became the first Eastern school to win the Orange Bowl since 1937 when the club rallied for a 15-14 victory.

720 The number of offensive plays (720) the Nittany Lions ran during the 2004 campaign. The offense averaged 4.7 yards per carry and averaged 310.7 yards per contest. On the other side of the football, the Penn State defense surrendered 291.5 yards per game.

721 The total number of punt and kickoff return yards (721) O.J. McDuffie accounted for during the 1992 season. McDuffie totaled 1,831 all-purpose yards, the second most in school history after Larry Johnson's 2,655 in 2002.

The number of passing yards (722) over the magical 1,000-yard mark compiled by Zack Mills during his 2004 senior season. The southpaw also ran for 72 yards with 13 total touchdowns.

The number of rushing yards (723) D.J. Dozier gained during the 1985 season. Dozier averaged 4.7 yards per carry and scored four touchdowns on the ground. The running back shared the November 11, 1985 cover of *Sports Illustrated* with Florida's Ray McDonald.

The approximate number of miles (724) between Penn State's campus in University Park, PA and Nashville, TN. Mike Reid, the 1969 Outland Trophy winner, played five seasons with the Cincinnati Bengals before his love of music led to retirement from football and a 1983 Grammy Award for his composition *Stranger in my House*. Reid lived in Nashville and was voted the Country Songwriter of the Year in 1985.

The day and year (7, '25) in November when Penn State hosted Notre Dame for Homecoming. The game ended in a scoreless tie and the Lions finished the season with a 4-4-1 record.

The number of receiving yards (726) Eric McCoo collected during his collegiate career. McCoo also added 192 return yards to his receiving and rushing totals, good for 3,436 all-purpose yards.

The number of football fans (727) over the 57,000 spectator mark on hand to watch Penn State and Arizona State duel in the 1977 Fiesta Bowl. It was a record crowd at the time, and the crowd witnessed Penn State get on the scoreboard first thanks to Joe Lally's 21-yard return off a blocked punt. PSU won the contest by a final of 42-30.

The number of rushing yards (728) Blair Thomas gained during his 1991 season with the New York Jets. Thomas also scored three of his seven career touchdowns that season. New York's first-round draft choice out of Penn State had a relatively disappointing career with just 2,236 rushing yards over six seasons. He entered the NFL with high expectations after finishing second to Houston quarterback Andre Ware in the 1989 Heisman Trophy voting.

729 The number of receiving yards (728) tight end Kyle Brady racked up during his 2000 campaign with the Jacksonville Jaguars. Brady's best season included a career high 64 catches and three touchdowns. The New Cumberland, PA native won the Red Worrell Award in 1993 as the most improved offensive player in spring practice at Penn State.

730 The combined number of total offensive yards (730) accumulated by Penn State and Tennessee in the 2007 Outback Bowl. Penn State racked up 380 total yards, while giving up 350 total yards to the Volunteers on January 1, 2007. Tony Hunt ran for 158 yards in Penn State's 20-10 victory.

731 The number of points and the year (7, '31) in which Penn State held Waynesburg to only seven points in the 1931 season opener. Unfortunately they were enough, as the Nittany Lions lost 7-0 to open a dreadful 2-8 campaign.

732 The winning percentage (.732) for head coach Bill Hollenback in 1909 and from 1911-14. Hollenback finished with a 28-9-4 record over five seasons. He coached the Nittany Lions in 1909 then served as Missouri's head coach before returning to Happy Valley for a four-year run as head man.

733 The non-conference winning percentage (.733) for the Big Ten during the 2006 season. The Nittany Lions won three of the conference's 33 non-conference contests, downing Akron, Youngstown State, and Temple.

734 The number of career return yards (734) piled up by Blair Thomas. The running back made an impact on kickoff returns during his 1986 sophomore season. Thomas' 91-yard return for a touchdown against Pittsburgh highlighted a solid season on special teams.

735 The season touchdown passing percentage (7.35) posted by John Hufnagel during the 1971 season. The McKees Rocks, PA native's 151.84 efficiency rating in 1971 is topped only by Kerry Collins' 172.86 rating in 1994.

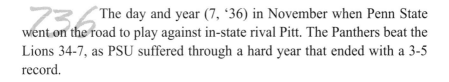 The day and year (7, '36) in November when Penn State went on the road to play against in-state rival Pitt. The Panthers beat the Lions 34-7, as PSU suffered through a hard year that ended with a 3-5 record.

The total number of offensive yards (737) put together by Elwood Petchel during his 1948 senior campaign. Petchel threw for 628 yards and nine touchdowns on 48 of 100 passing. He even excelled on defense and special teams, bringing back 14 punts for 144 yards and intercepting four passes.

The number of points and the year (7, '38) in which Penn State scored only seven points against Penn during its 1938 game. The Lion defense held though, and the teams played to a 7-7 tie. PSU closed out the season, however, with a 26-0 loss at the hands of #5 Pitt and an overall record of just 3-4-1.

The number of rushing yards (739) Eric McCoo gained during the 1999 season. The Red Bank, NJ native averaged 5.0 yards per carry and rushed for four touchdowns in his junior season. His collegiate stats opened several professional doors and McCoo walked through overseas. He was allocated by the Philadelphia Eagles to Berlin in 2003 and won MVP of World Bowl XII.

The number of receiving yards (740) amassed by Baltimore, MD native Bryant Johnson during his 2006 season with the Arizona Cardinals. Johnson's play at Penn State convinced the Cardinals to make him their first-round pick in the 2003 draft. He came into his own with a career-high four touchdown grabs during his fourth year in the NFL.

The season touchdown pass percentage (7.41) for Pete Liske during the 1962 campaign. The accurate and intelligent signal caller was careful with the football and finished his collegiate career with a 127.71 passing efficiency.

The number of Division I head coaching changes (742) from Joe Paterno's first season in 1966 up until Penn State gave him a new four-year contract extension in May 2004. Every other Division I institution averaged six head coaches over that period.

743 The number of all-purpose yards (743) Ki-Jana Carter racked up over the 1,000-yard mark during his 1994 senior season. Carter sprinted for three touchdowns of 80-plus yards during the campaign, and he led the conference in rushing, scoring, and all-purpose yards.

744 The overall career winning percentage (.744) for Joe Paterno through the 2007 season. Paterno's 372 victories place him one behind Florida State head coach Bobby Bowden for the all-time wins mark.

745 The number of all-purpose yards (745) gained by Tony Orsini during the 1950 season. Orsini added to his rushing total with 153 return yards and 29 receiving yards.

746 The number of rushing yards (746) Texas A&M running back Jorvorskie Lane compiled going into the 2007 Alamo Bowl against Penn State's run-stuffing front seven. The Nittany Lions held the bowling ball shaped back to just 34 yards on 10 carries.

747 The number of Maxwell Award points (747) Colorado running back Eric Bieniemy received in the 1990 race won by Brigham Young quarterback Ty Detmer. The Maxwell Club also announced that Joe Paterno won the George Munger Award as the outstanding college coach.

748 The number of wins and the year (7, '48) in which Penn State went 7-1-1 under Coach Bob Higgins.

749 The average yards per pass (7.49) for each Kevin Thompson completion during his collegiate career. Thompson and Chafie Fields connected for one of the longest pass plays in program history, a 78-yard strike in 1999 at Purdue.

750 The number of carries (750) running back Evan Royster logged during his distinguished high school career. Royster sprinted for

6,384 yards and 90 total touchdowns at Westfield High School in Chantilly, VA before contributing during his freshman season in Happy Valley.

751 The number of rushing yards (751) Lydell Mitchell gained as a junior in 1970. Mitchell carried the football 134 times and also returned 16 kickoffs for 410 yards.

752 The number of wins and the year (7, '52) Penn State went 7-2-1 under Coach Rip Engle and cracked the AP Top 15 that season.

753 The season touchdown pass percentage (7.53) posted by Todd Blackledge during the 1982 season. The Academic All-American threw four touchdowns in a game three times during the 1982 campaign (Temple, Maryland, and Rutgers).

754 The number of wins and the year (7, '54) Penn State went 7-2 under Coach Rip Engle and a #20 AP ranking.

755 The number of points and the year (7, '55) in which Penn State scored only seven points against #8 West Virginia in 1955. The Mountaineers won the game 21-7 at home in Morgantown, WV. PSU won their next three games, however, to secure a winning record of 5-4 on the season.

756 The number of rushing yards (756) over the 1,000-yard mark Richie Anderson amassed during his four-season stay in Happy Valley. Anderson navigated his way into the end zone 29 times on 363 rushing attempts.

757 The number of yards (757) traveled by Ralph Giacomarro's 18 punts during his 1987 season with the Denver Broncos. The punter played in the NFL for the Atlanta Falcons from 1983-85 before joining the Broncos in 1987. He punted the football 185 times over those four seasons with a 41.0 yard-per-punt average. Giacomarro averaged 43.6 yards per punt for the Nittany Lions during the 1981 campaign.

758 The number of points and the year (7, '58) in which Penn State scored only seven points in their 1958 season opener against Nebraska. The Cornhuskers won the game 14-7, and the Nittany Lions went on to lose two out of three to start the season. Despite the poor start, PSU recovered and posted an overall 6-3-1 mark that included a 25-21 road victory against Pitt.

759 The number of points and the year (7, '59) in which Penn State scored only 7 points against Alabama in the 1959 Liberty Bowl. But the Lion defense held up, and the #14 Lions rolled to a 7-0 victory against the #11 Crimson Tide.

760 The winning percentage (.760) of head coach George W. Hoskins from 1892-95. Hoskins was hired as the first "official" head football coach and the first director of physical training in January 1892. The Nittany Lions (6-0-1) finished unbeaten for the first time in 1894, and Hoskins resigned in the summer of 1896 to take the head coaching position at Pittsburgh.

761 The approximate number of miles (761) between Penn State's campus in University Park, PA and the home of the Bryan Scott "Pick Your Passion" Foundation for the Arts in Atlanta, GA. Scott recorded 202 tackles at Penn State before heading to the Atlanta Falcons in the second round of the 2003 NFL draft. Other than football, Scott's passion at a young age was music. He played piano, drums, and saxophone as a kid, and he performed with recording artist Michelle Branch on Monday Night Football's music competition "Monday Night at the Mic" in 2003.

762 The number of points and the year (7, '62) in which Penn State scored only 7 points against Florida in the 1962 Gator Bowl in Jacksonville. The Lions came into the contest #9 in the country, but lost 17-7 to the unranked Gators.

763 Penn State's winning percentage (.763) from 2005-07. The 29-9 record is tied with Auburn for the 13th best mark nationally over the three-year period.

764 The number of rushing yards (764) totaled by Kansas City Chiefs running back Marcus Allen in 1993 behind an offensive line anchored by former Penn State standout Dave Szott. The burly beast in the trenches enjoyed a 13-year NFL career with the Chiefs and New York Jets after a successful collegiate career that included blocking for Blair Thomas in 1987 and 1989.

765 The number of college coaching changes (765) between Joe Paterno's first season in 1966 and the 2005 season. Paterno has been the head coach through 61 Big Ten coaching changes, including eight at Illinois and Michigan State through the 2005 campaign.

766 The combined number of rushing yards and rushing touchdowns (766) totaled by running back Leroy Thompson during his 1993 season with the Pittsburgh Steelers. He amassed 763 yards and scored three touchdowns. Thompson played three of his six NFL seasons in the Steel City, with one each in Kansas City, New England, and Tampa Bay. One of Thompson's best collegiate games came when he scored four touchdowns in a 28-0 rout of Rutgers in 1990.

767 The career touchdown pass percentage (7.67) posted by Tom Shuman. First and foremost, Shuman was a winner, leading the Nittany Lions to victory in 22 of his 24 starts, with the two defeats by a total of six points. He threw 28 career touchdowns to just 12 interceptions.

768 The average yards per pass (7.68) for each of Chuck Fusina's pass completions during the 1978 campaign. He connected on 15 of 29 passes for 234 yards, including a 63-yard touchdown pass to Tom Donovan, in one of his better collegiate games against unbeaten Maryland that November.

769 The draft pick and year (7, '69) PSU tight end Ted Kwalick was selected by the San Francisco 49ers with the seventh overall pick in the 1969 NFL/AFL draft. Five PSU players were selected in that year's draft.

770   The combined number of rushing yards and rushing touchdowns (770) for Kenny Watson during his 2007 NFL season as a member of the Cincinnati Bengals. He tallied 763 rushing yards and seven rushing touchdowns. Cincinnati called Watson's number 178 times—his highest total to date—and the running back answered with 4.3 yards per attempt. The former PSU back ran for 34 yards and caught 16 passes, good for 275 yards and two touchdowns, during his senior season in 2000.

771   The AP ranking and year (#7, '71) #7 Penn State played Texas Christian University in their 1971 Homecoming game. Penn State won the game 66-14. The Lions ended the year at 11-1 with a #5 AP ranking.

772   The number of all-time victories (772) posted by the Nittany Lions heading into a September 9, 2006, contest at Notre Dame. The Fighting Irish, owners of 813 victories, won the historic heavyweight bout, 41-17. Anthony Morelli threw for 189 yards and Tony Hunt added 74 on the ground in defeat.

773   The number of college football fans (773) over the 77,000 spectator mark that watched Kevin Kelly's game-winning 29-yard field goal in the third overtime of the 2006 Orange Bowl. Austin Scott supported Penn State's cause with 110 rushing yards and two touchdowns in place of an injured Tony Hunt.

774   The AP and Coaches polls ranking (7, '74) of #7 PSU at the end of the 1974 season after the Nittany Lions pasted Baylor 41-20 in the Cotton Bowl. The Lions ended the year at 10-2.

775   The combined number of total yards and touchdowns (775) quarterback Chuck Burkhart accounted for during the 1969 season. Burkhart posted 773 total yards and accounted for two touchdowns. He ended the season with an 11 of 26 passing effort against Missouri in a 10-3 1970 Orange Bowl victory.

776   The career field goal percentage (77.6) for Nick Gancitano—a Penn State career record. Gancitano converted 38 of 49 field goal attempts from 1981-83.

The team leading number of rushing yards (777) gained by Tony Hunt during the 2004 season. Hunt's number was called 169 times, and he answered with seven touchdowns and 70.6 rushing yards per contest.

The number of passes (778) attempted by Pete Liske during his five-year NFL career with the New York Jets, the Denver Broncos, and the Philadelphia Eagles. Liske completed 396 passes for 5,170 yards, 30 touchdowns, and 46 interceptions. The quarterback and defensive back also played professionally in Canada with Calgary, where he was named the CFL's Most Valuable Player in 1967. Liske was named All-East as a Nittany Lion in 1963.

The number of rushing yards (779) Richie Anderson gained during the 1991 season. The Sandy Spring, MD product also caught 21 passes for 255 yards, and returned 9 kickoffs for 222 yards as a junior.

The number of victories (780) totaled by the Nittany Lions in their first 120 years of football through the 2006 season. Penn State posted a record of 780-343-42, and then added a 9-4 mark to that total in 2007. The Nittany Lions began the 2007 campaign tied with Alabama for sixth nationally in all-time victories.

The AP ranking and the year (#7, '81) in which #7 Penn State played their final game against USC in the 1982 Fiesta Bowl. Penn State won the game 26-10 on New Year's Day and ended the season at 10-2.

The number of total tackles (782) credited to the Penn State defense during the 2004 season. Paul Posluszny's 104 tackles outdistanced fellow linebacker Dan Connor's 85, and safety Andrew Guman's 67 total stops.

The overall draft pick and year (7, '83) that PSU quarterback Todd Blackledge was selected by the Kansas City Chiefs with the seventh overall pick in the 1983 NFL draft. That same year Blackledge won the Davey O'Brien Award for the nation's top play caller.

784 The number of first place votes (784) Southern California running back Reggie Bush totaled in his 2005 Heisman Trophy winning season, 782 more than Penn State quarterback Michael Robinson. The signal caller also garnered seven second place votes and 29 third place votes to finish fifth in the balloting.

785 The season touchdown pass percentage (7.85) credited to quarterback Kevin Thompson during the 1999 season. Thompson completed 55% of his passes and threw 13 touchdown passes on only 242 attempts.

786 The number of career punt return yards (786) piled up by Bobby Engram during his collegiate career—a number only surpassed by O.J. McDuffie's 1,059 punt return yards. Engram averaged 12.2 yards on 33 punt returns during his sophomore season.

787 The draft round pick and year (7, '87) that Penn State tight end Brian Siverling was selected by the Detroit Lions with the 7th pick of round 11 in the 1987 NFL draft. Penn State had a total of 13 players selected in the 1987 draft.

788 The passing yards average (7.88) for each of Tom Sherman's completions during the 1967 season. He threw four touchdown passes in a 42-6 win over Pittsburgh as part of a 14-touchdown campaign—a record he held for 10 years.

789 The number of victories (789) in the program's history through the 2007 season. The Nittany Lions have averaged just over 6.5 victories per season in their 120 year history, dating back to 1887.

790 The number of receiving yards (790) O.J. McDuffie recorded during the 1991 season. The Gates Mills, Ohio native also ran for 107 yards, and totaled a team best 1,367 all-purpose yards.

791 The number of passes (791) attempted by Anthony Morelli going into his final collegiate game against Texas A&M. He added 31 to that number in the victory over the Aggies, completing 15 of those

throws while his backup Daryll Clark made an appearance as a running threat. Clark carried the football 6 times for 50 yards.

Penn State's winning percentage (.792) during offensive lineman Keith Dorney's decorated collegiate career (1975-78). Dorney was twice named to the All-American team, earning a unanimous selection in 1978. The Detroit Lions made him the 10th selection in the 1979 NFL draft, and he played his entire NFL career in the Motor City through 1987. The offensive lineman was inducted into the National Football Foundation College Football Hall of Fame in December 2005.

The number of offensive plays (793) the Nittany Lions ran during the 2003 season. The offense averaged 4.7 yards per play and 313.3 yards per contest. On the other side of the football, Penn State's defense allowed an average of 362.4 yards per game—and the difference contributed to a shocking 3-9 record.

The number of times and the year (7, '94) in which PSU scored at least 40 points seven times during 1994 en route to a 12-0 record. Although PSU ended the season unbeaten and untied, the NCAA saw fit to bestow a #2 ranking on the Lions.

The season touchdown pass percentage (7.95) posted by signal caller Kerry Collins during his historic 1994 season. Collins also set the school record for passing efficiency at 172.86, which was just four points shy of the NCAA record.

The number of all-purpose yards (796) pieced together by running back D.J. Dozier during the 1984 season. Dozier did most of his damage from the backfield, navigating his way around, past, and through defenders to the tune of 691 yards. He also added 55 return yards and 50 receiving yards over the course of the campaign.

The draft round and year (7, '97) PSU quarterback Wally Richardson was selected by the Baltimore Ravens in seventh round of the 1997 NFL Draft. Richardson was selected as the 234th overall pick.

798 PSU played seven games in front of 95,000 plus fans in 1998 (7,'98)-including an ABC televised game against Michigan in Ann Arbor that was witnessed firsthand by more than 111,000 fans. The Nittany Lions came away disappointed, however, after losing the game 27-0. They were more fortunate in the other six contests in front of legions of Penn State faithful. Routs of Southern Mississippi and Bowling Green began a promising campaign and home victories over Purde and Illinois preceded the loss to the Wolverines. Two more home victories over Northwestern and Michigan State propelled the Nittany Lions to an 8-3 regular season. The 26-14 Outback Bowl victory over Kentucky was played in front of just over 66,000 spectators at Tampa's Raymond James Stadium.

799 The number of career receiving yards (799) totaled by running back Tony Hunt. The powerhouse between the tackles caught 88 passes with three touchdowns from 2003-06. The Alexandria, Virginia native was drafted by the Philadelphia Eagles in the third round of the 2007 NFL draft. Hunt saw limited action as a rookie with the Eagles in 2007, carrying the ball just ten times for 16 yards. His first career touch came in a 56-21 victory over the Detroit Lions in the Eagles third game of the season-but it resulted in a loss of three yards. He got four carries on the day, the second of which was a gain of three yards, and with his third touch he was able to punch it into the end zone from one yard out for his first career NFL touchdown. Hunt did not catch an NFL pass until week one of the 2008 season, when he also scored his second career rushing touchdown in a 38-3 victory over the Rams.

800 The total number of combined yards (800) accumulated by Florida State and Penn State in the 1990 Blockbuster Bowl. The inaugural bowl game was dead even on the stat sheet with each team posting 400 total yards. However, a partially blocked punt and a blocked field goal hurt Penn State's chances in a 24-17 defeat that pitted legendary head coaches Joe Paterno and Bobby Bowden against each other. The two names have been synonomous with college football for over half a century, justling for position at the top of the all-time wins list to this day. For all of their similarities on the field and their close friendship off it, the two coaching icons currently have very different answers to the retirement question. Bowden already has a succession plan in place at Florida State, where offensive coordinator Jimbo Fisher will take over once the Seminoles icon decides to call it quits. When asked at a press conference when he may step aside, Paterno's tone scolded the question as he said, "I don't know. How many times can I say it?"

Penn State Nittany Lions, 1954 Schedule

Opponent	Result
at Illinois	W 14-12
at Syracuse	W 13-0
Virginia	W 34-7
West Virginia	L 14-19
at Texas Christian	L 7-20
at Pennsylvania	W 35-13
Holy Cross	W 39-7
Rutgers	W 37-14
at Pittsburgh	W 13-0

Teamwork is the ability to work together toward a common vision. The ability to direct individual accomplishment toward organizational objectives. It is the fuel that allows common people to attain uncommon results.

—*Andrew Carnegie*

Chapter Nine

The Do-Everything Nittany Lion

*J*ack of all trades, master of none. The phrase coined to describe a player adequate in many facets of competition, but lacking supreme talent in one area of the game, is an insult in its current form.

However, that doesn't describe Penn State passer, runner, and kicker Don Bailey. The Pittsburgh native grew up with soot on his hands and football in his heart. Talent accompanied a strong work ethic, leading to a prominent role on Rip Engle's 1952 squad.

He served as the team's main punt return threat, opening eyes with a 77-yard gallop for a touchdown at Syracuse, and setting up Penn State's first touchdown in a 20-13 victory over Temple earlier that season. In total, Bailey returned 16 punts for 213 yards, and also stamped his place in Penn State's rotation as a steady defensive back, spurring the Nittany Lions to a 10-0 Homecoming victory over Nebraska with an end zone interception.

Bailey was thrust into the role of multi-unit star thanks in part to a rule change prior to the 1953 season. The rule stated that a player who played during a quarter and left the field could not come back into the game until a subsequent quarter, except in the final four minutes of the second and fourth periods when a player was allowed to return if he had already played in that current quarter.

In pigskin terms—wiping away the convoluted rules-speak of football's governing body—it meant that players would play both ways, and kickers would have to learn the basic fundamentals of blocking and tackling, or ride the pine.

And so began Bailey's legend. A rule change turned him from a backup quarterback with punt returning skills to a do-everything star with the instincts and athleticism to excel on offense, defense, and special teams.

He sat in the background absorbing the intricacies of each position and bulking up to better absorb the physicality of the college game. Lenny Moore stole the show as a ball carrier and a defensive back, earning the nickname "The Reading Express" for the Nittany Lions (6-3).

Starting quarterback Tony Rados was lost to graduation, leaving a cavernous hole under center as Penn State prepared for the 1954 season. Joe Paterno didn't envision Don Bailey as the heir apparent, urging Engle to start sophomore Milt Plum instead.

"I didn't want to use him (Bailey)," Paterno recalled in his book, *Football My Way*. "You never knew what he was going to do."

Paterno thought Bailey's book was already written. He saw the senior as a solid defensive back, a fine punter, and an adequate runner, but a sight for sore eyes when it came to tossing a spiral out wide. Plum also struggled in the preseason, and Engle tabbed junior Bobby Hoffman the starting quarterback by default for the season opener against Illinois.

He instituted the quarterback option prior to the contest, providing another opportunity to get the dynamic Moore out in space. The move would prove to be genius in time.

An early Hoffman interception gave the heavily favored Illini an early advantage, and Engle threw caution to the wind. He brought in Bailey. Like the new option package, the move to Bailey would work in time. After a punt and an interception, Bailey threw a 24-yard touchdown pass to Jesse Arnelle, and later sprinted around the left end for 50 yards as part of a drive that concluded with a Bailey-to-Moore option and another touchdown.

The upset over Illinois and a victory over Syracuse gave Engle reason for optimism. "I now have confidence in this team, and even more important, I think our players have confidence in themselves," Engle told the *Centre-Daily Times*. "I believe we have a good chance in every game."

The Nittany Lions fell in heartbreaking fashion to West Virginia, and then dropped an error-riddled decision to Texas Christian—but that was it, they did not lose again the rest of the season.

Penn State dominated Pittsburgh, 13-0, with Bailey—the option signal caller so vital to Moore's success—scoring the final touchdown on a three-yard burst up the middle.

Bailey finished the season with 393 passing yards, five touchdowns, and just two interceptions. He also led the team in punting with 26 boots for 898 yards and a 34.5-yard average.

Most importantly, he was the man who got the ball into Moore's hands. He understood his strengths and his limitations. He was athletically sound and intellectually gifted.

He was a track of all trades . . . yet, the full quote better describes Bailey's collegiate career. "Jack of all trades, master of none, though oft times better than master of one."

The time and year (8, '01) in which Penn State scheduled an 8:00 pm kickoff to open the 2001 season against the Miami Hurricanes on September 1. The game was televised by ABC and 109,313 fans were on hand to witness a Hurricane come through PA as PSU lost 33-7.

The month and year (8, '02) that Penn State opened its season against the University of Central Florida. The August 31 match-up was televised by ESPN and another 103,029 fans watched the game from University Park as the Lions beat the Knights 27-24.

The month and year (8, '03) that Penn State opened its season against Temple. The August 30 match-up was televised by ESPN

Plus and another 101,553 PSU crazies watched the game from University Park as the Lions beat the Owls 23-10.

The number of Big Ten games played and the year (8, '04) that Penn State faced eight conference opponents during 2004. Things did not go well, however, as the Nittany Lions posted only a 2-6 conference record and struggled to a 4-7 mark overall.

The time and year (8, '05) when the Nittany Lions met Florida State for an 8:00 pm to end the 2005 season at the Orange Bowl. The game was televised by ABC, and 77,773 fans were on hand to witness a thrilling triple overtime 26-23 victory for PSU.

The number of rushing yards (806) gained by starting quarterback Michael Robinson during the 2005 season. Robinson also led the team with 11 rushing scores and averaged 4.9 yards per carry.

The time and year (8, '07) when Penn State met Texas A&M for an 8:00 pm kickoff in the 2007 Alamo Bowl in San Antonio. The game was televised by ESPN and 66,166 fans were on hand to witness a 24-17 PSU win.

The single season touchdown pass percentage record (8.08) set by Tom Shuman in 1973. Shuman completed 83 passes on 161 attempts with 13 of those completions going for touchdowns.

The number of rushing yards (809) Penn State running back Rodney Kinlaw amassed through the Ohio State game during the 2007 season. At the time, Kinlaw was averaging 5.2 yards per carry. In the October 27 loss to then No. 2 Ohio State, Kinlaw collected 81 yards for 5.8 yards per carry.

The number of rushing yards (810) gained by PSU's Devin Fentress during his 2004 senior year at Western Branch High School. As a running back, Fentress scored nine touchdowns while leading WBHS to three district titles. He made the leap to PSU and played in his first collegiate game against Illinois in 2005 as a cornerback. That day, Fentress had three solo tackles and one pass breakup.

811 The number of Heisman Trophy ballots (811) that were returned by voters during the 2002 selection. There were 921 ballots sent out to voters and 88% of those were returned. Penn State's running back Larry Johnson finished third in the voting behind USC quarterback Carson Palmer and Iowa quarterback Brad Banks.

812 The number of punt return yards (812) gained by Penn State's Calvin Lowry during his 39 career games wearing the blue and white. Lowry also snagged nine interceptions and was named to the first team All-Big Ten squad his senior season. Lowry was selected in the fourth round of the 2006 NFL draft by the Tennessee Titans.

813 The number of players (813) inducted into the College Football Hall of Fame before Joe Pa got the call himself in 2007. At the time, Coach Paterno was one of 174 coaches in the Hall. His class was inducted during a December 4, 2007 ceremony in New York City.

814 The area code (814) of the Penn State Athletic Ticket Office. The phone number to buy tickets for PSU games is (814) 863-1000. The address is 240 Bryce Jordan Center, University Park, PA 16802.

815 The field goal percentage (81.5) for kicker Matt Bahr during his 1978 All-American season, breaking his brother Chris' NCAA percentage record. Bahr split the uprights four times in four different games during that season, showcasing a right foot that won many games for six different NFL franchises over the course of a 17-year career.

816 The number of reception yards (816) collected in 2007 by A.J. Price during his senior prep campaign at South Lakes High School in Reston, Virginia. The 6' 4" receiver caught 32 passes and scored 11 touchdowns before signing with Penn State.

817 The number of receiving yards (817) compiled by wide receiver Joe Jurevicius during his senior season in 1997. Jurevicius caught a team leading 39 passes with 10 touchdowns and was a second-team All-Big Ten performer. The 1997 Biletnikoff Award semifinalist finished his stay in Happy Valley with 94 receptions, 1,894 yards, and 15 scores. He finished his career fourth on Penn State's career receiving list.

818 The average number of alcoholic drinks (8.18) consumed by Penn State students during the weekend as reported by a 2004 Penn State Pulse survey. In 2006, it increased to 9.59 drinks during the weekend. The survey did not say if this was a result of PSU winning or losing!

819 The preseason Power Rating (.819) for the 1997 Nittany Lions. Penn State finished the year with an overall 9-3 record and an invite to play Florida in the Citrus Bowl, a game it lost 21-6.

820 The number of chair-back seats (820) inserted at Beaver Stadium in the first five rows of a deck constructed in the north end zone prior to the 1990 season. The seats were sold for $30 per game.

821 The number of passing yards (821) racked up by Tony Sacca as a freshman in 1988. Sacca capped his career with a season to remember in 1991, throwing for 2,488 yards and 21 touchdowns to just five interceptions.

822 The team best number of rushing yards (822) for Eric McCoo during the 1998 season. The running back had a rare combination of power and deceptive speed, making him difficult to bring down between the tackles or around the edge. McCoo averaged 6.5 yards per carry with three touchdowns in 1998.

823 The number of snaps (823) that linebacker Sean Lee saw during his 2006 sophomore season at Penn State. The Pittsburgh, PA native from Upper St. Clair was an Academic All-Big Ten selection and Finance major.

824 The number of passes (824) attempted by PSU quarterback Tony Sacca from 1988-91. Sacca completed 401 of those attempts while collecting 5,869 yards through the air. Sacca also threw for 41 touchdowns.

825 The combined number of solo tackles and sacks (82.5) for defensive nose guard Brandon Noble during his collegiate career. He notched 69 tackles and 13.5 sacks. Joe Paterno called him "the best nose guard in the country" for his excellence on the field, and in the locker room, on the 1996 team. Noble started every game as a junior and senior, and finished his career with 147 tackles.

826 The height in inches (8.26) of *The Lion in Autumn*. The book's dimensions are 8.26 x 5.23 inches, and it is 336 pages long. The book was written by Frank Fitzpatrick, a *Philadelphia Inquirer* sportswriter. *Publishers Weekly* calls the book "a biography of Paterno-and thus a biography of Penn State football as it is known today."

827 The number of reception yards (827) collected on 39 passes by former Nittany Lion Anwar Phillips during his senior season at Northwest High School in Germantown, Maryland. He became a two-time All-Big Ten selection at cornerback for Penn State, and on January 30, 2006, while playing in the 57th Senior Bowl, he made two tackles and returned an interception for 49 yards, helping the North beat the South 31-14. He has since suited up in the NFL for the Baltimore Ravens and the New Orleans Saints.

828 The number of times (828) Matt Suhey carried the football during his NFL career with the Chicago Bears from 1980-89. Suhey's best season came as the team's fullback in 1983, when he rushed for a career high 681 yards and caught 49 passes for 429 yards. The second-round draft pick out of Penn State was part of the 1985 Super Bowl champion Bears.

829 The number of players (829) enshrined as of 2008 in the College Football Hall of Fame. Penn State has supplied 21 of those members thus far!

830 The month and day (8, 30) PSU opened the 2008 season against Coastal Carolina. The Nittany Lions 2008 schedule had four home games in five to start the season: Coastal Carolina; Oregon State; at Syracuse; Temple; and Illinois.

831 The number of losses and the year (8, '31) in which Penn State suffered eight losses during the 1931 season under head coach Bob Higgins. The team ended the season with a dismal 2-8 showing overall. The season was bad, but if there was a high note, it was the season-ending 31-0 triumph over Lehigh in Philadelphia.

832 The number of yards (832) Gary Wydman threw for during the 1964 season. Wydman completed 70 of 149 passes for the Nittany Lions, who closed the season with five straight victories to post a 6-4 record. One of those wins came in Columbus against #2 Ohio State.

833 The winning percentage (.833) for the 1981 Penn State squad. The Nittany Lions finished the season with a 10-2 record, a Fiesta Bowl invite, and an AP and Coaches #3 ranking.

834 The number of offensive plays (834) run by the Penn State offense in 2005. The Nittany Lions averaged 6.1 yards per play and 421.5 yards of total offense per contest. On the other side of the football, the defense allowed just 4.2 yards per play and 304.7 total yards per game.

835 The number of views (835) on You Tube's "Penn State Football at THON 2008" as of June 8, 2008. The Penn State Football team danced a hilarious rendition of the Macarena to the song "MMMBop" for a great cause. Go to YouTube.com and check it out.

836 The preseason Power Rating (.836) of the 1976 Penn State squad. The Lions finished the season with a 7-5 record and an invitation to a Gator Bowl meeting with the Fighting Irish from Notre Dame.

837 The final Power Rating (.837) of the 1975 Penn State team. The Lions finished the season with an overall record of 9-3, a Sugar Bowl invite, and an AP and Coaches ranking of #10.

838 The day and year (8, '38) in October when Penn State played its annual Homecoming game. Unfortunately for the home team, the Lions lost to Bucknell by a score of 14-0.

The number of games and the year PSU took the field eight times during 1939 (8, '39) and posted a 5-1-2 record. The season ended on a high note as the club beat Pittsburgh 10-0 at New Beaver Field.

The number of passing yards (840) for Doug Strang during his senior season. Strang threw 10 touchdowns to five interceptions in 1984 after a 1983 campaign that included seven touchdown passes and 1,944 yards through the air. The signal caller threw for 2,966 yards with 24 touchdown passes from 1981-84.

The number of snaps (841) Levi Brown participated in during his 2003 season with the Nittany Lions. Brown started all 12 games at left tackle during the campaign.

The ticket markup (842%) by one savvy Penn State student for the November 18, 2006 game vs. Michigan State. The student bought his seat for $190 and then jacked up the price to $1,600 to take advantage of the big demand for tickets. The student listed the seat at Craigslist, an online auction site. To get around scalping laws, the student sold an overpriced pen and gave the tickets away for free—a brilliant con!

The number of reception yards (843) on 39 catches by Penn State's Andrew Quarless during his junior prep season at Uniondale High School in New York in 2004. The All-League selection faired well on the other side of the ball by pulling down 50 tackles and 16 sacks that same season.

The passer rating (84.4) of Pennsylvania native and NFL Hall of Famer Jim Kelly during his NFL career. The five-time Pro Bowler's roots are deep in East Brady, PA, and he was recruited by Penn State to play linebacker before he opted for Miami, the quarterback position, and the sunshine. In his first college start with the Hurricanes, Kelly led Miami to an upset victory over Penn State. He then went on to post a 20-6 career mark with the Hurricanes.

The percentage (84.5) of Fantasy League Football owners who owned Larry Johnson during the 2007 season according to

ESPN.com. That percentage is a credit to Johnson's potential ability to gain yards and score TDs.

846 The number of receiving yards (846) piled up by wide receiver Terry Smith during the 1991 season. Smith totaled 55 catches and averaged 15.4 yards each time he hauled in a pass. The former Penn State wide receiver is the current head coach at Gateway High School, and was instrumental in guiding his stepson and former Gateway star Justin King to Happy Valley.

847 The number of rushing yards per game (84.7) surrendered by the Nittany Lion defense during the first seven games of the 2006 season. That was until the Lions met the University of Illinois. The Fighting Illini racked up 202 yards on the ground during the October 21 meeting. PSU still won the game 26-12.

848 The day and year (8, '48) in November when the Lions met Temple on the road in front of 20,000 fans and escaped Philly with a 7-0 win.

849 The day and year (8, '49) in October when the Lions met Boston College in front of 18,041 fans. Penn State secured its first win of the season after handling BC 32-14.

850 The total number of rushing yards (850) for Dave Kasperian during the 1957 and 1958 seasons. Kasperian ran for 469 yards in 1957 and 381 yards in 1958, scoring seven and five touchdowns in the two seasons respectively. The Nittany Lions finished 6-3 in 1957 and sported a 6-3-1 mark one year later.

851 The month and year (8, '51) in which the *Syracuse Herald Journal* newspaper announced news that Texas Christian and Wisconsin were being added to the Nittany Lions' 1953 football schedule.

852 The day and year (8, '52) in November when the Nittany Lions traveled to Syracuse and lost 25-7 in front of 16,000 fans. It was PSU's second loss of the year, and it closed out the season at 7-2-1.

853 The month and year (8, '53) that the *Charleston Daily Mail* newspaper announced that Pitt and Penn State were the strongest non-league opponents after reviewing an Associated Press survey of major conference football teams. The AP survey looked at the conferences for a 25- year period from 1928 through 1952.

854 The RAT (85.4), or quarterback rating, of former Nittany Lion Kerry Collins during his 2002 season with the New York Giants. That year, Collins completed 335 of his 545 passes. The Lebanon, PA native's 2002 RAT is his highest to date.

855 The day and year (8, '55) in October when the Lions traveled to Richmond to play Virginia. Penn State beat the Cavaliers 26-7, and closed out the season with another winning record at 5-4.

856 The day and year (8, '56) in October when the Lions traveled to Army to take on the Cadets. The Black Knights won the game 14-7 and handed PSU its first loss of the season. Penn State still managed a winning season though and posted a 6-2-1 record.

857 The price ($8.57) of a USED-GOOD copy of *Tales from Penn State Football* by Ken Rappoport on amazon.com in May of 2008. The 192-page read by *Sports Publishing* takes an inside look at PSU Football.

858 The number of rushing yards (858) amassed by Dick Hoak during his 1968 All-Pro season with the Pittsburgh Steelers. Hoak played all 10 of his professional campaigns with the Steelers, rushing for 3,965 yards and 25 touchdowns after a quiet, but productive collegiate career in Happy Valley.

859 The final Power Rating (.859) for PSU during the 1985 season. The squad finished with an 11-1 record and ranked fourth behind only Michigan, Oklahoma, and Tennessee in the Power Ratings.

860 The number of receiving yards (860) piled up by split end Greg Edmonds from 1968-70. Edmonds caught 66 passes for six touchdowns. He led the team in receiving during his senior season with six touchdowns, which at that time was a single season record.

861   The number of reception yards (861) collected by two-year starter Tony Stewart during his stay with the Blue and White. As a senior, Stewart set a Lions record for most catches in a season by a tight end with 38 catches for 451 yards. That season, Stewart earned 2000 *Football News* honorable mention All-American honors.

862   The average number of all-purpose yards (86.2) gained per game by Derrick Williams during the 2007 season. Williams played in all 13 games and picked up 101 rushing yards, 529 receiving yards, 253 punt return yards, and 237 kick return yards. His 1,121 yards gained were second only to Rodney Kinlaw's 1,475 all-purpose yards.

863   The month and year (8, '63) that former Navy Midshipman quarterback George Welsh was named as a Penn State assistant coach according to the *Nevada State Journal* newspaper.

864   The number of points and year (8, '64) when Penn State scored eight points during its 1964 season opener—a 21-8 loss to the Midshipmen of Navy. Although the Nittany Lions started the season with four losses in their first five games, they still managed a winning season at 6-4.

865   The final Power Rating (.865) for the Penn State Nittany Lions during the 1991 season. The team finished with an 11-2 record and ranked third only behind undefeated Washington and Miami in the Power Ratings.

866   The month and year (8, '66), according to the *Bucks County Courier Times* newspaper, that Penn State started accepting ticket orders for the upcoming season. Reserved seats for Joe Pa's first game against Maryland: $5. PSU won the game 15-7.

867   The number of wins and the year (8, '67) when Penn State posted eight victories in 1967 despite losing to Navy to start the season.

PSU was able to turn things around, post an 8-2-1 record, notch a bid to the Gator Bowl, and earn a final AP ranking of #10.

868 The month and year (8, '68), according to the *Valley Independent* newspaper, that members of the Eastern Association of Intercollegiate Football Officials met at Penn State for their annual clinic. These officials conducted instructional sessions and discussions on rule interpretations from August 22-24, 1968.

869 The career number of average yards-per-attempt (8.69) for quarterback John Hufnagel. The heady and talented signal caller threw for 3,545 yards with 26 touchdowns and only 17 interceptions from 1970-72.

870 The month and year (8, '70) that the *Iowa City Press Citizen* announced Penn State's biggest threat to winning a fourth consecutive Lambert Trophy was West Virginia. PSU didn't win its fourth straight in 1970, but neither did WVU. That honor went to Dartmouth.

871 The month and year (8, '71) that the *Daily Herald* newspaper announced Penn State and Tennessee's December 1 meeting in Knoxville would be the last televised game of the regular season. It ended up being PSU's only loss of the year — a 31-11 loss to the Vols.

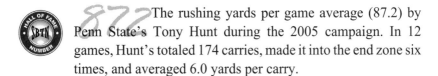 *872* The rushing yards per game average (87.2) by Penn State's Tony Hunt during the 2005 campaign. In 12 games, Hunt's totaled 174 carries, made it into the end zone six times, and averaged 6.0 yards per carry.

873 The number of receiving yards (873) Bobby Engram totaled during the 1993 season. Engram caught more passes and racked up more yards in each of his next two campaigns, but 1993 will be remembered as the season he found the end zone. He reached the ultimate destination a total of 13 times on 48 receptions.

874 The month and year (8, '74), according to the *Bucks County Courier Times*, that the Lions announced six of their assistant coaches for the upcoming year would be graduates of Penn State. PSU—keeping it all in the family.

875 The average rushing yards per game (87.5) by PSU opponents during the 2006 season. On the other side of the line, Penn State gained 150 yards per game on the ground while outscoring opponents 290-187.

876 The month and year (8, '76) that the *Portsmouth Herald* stated the incoming freshman class is "the best crop of freshman talent ever recruited at Penn State." That may have been true. In 1977 and 1978, PSU combined for only two losses.

877 The number of offensive plays (877) run by the Nittany Lions during the 2002 season. The offense averaged 6.3 yards per play and 423.7 yards per game. On the other side of the football, the Nittany Lion defense allowed 4.6 yards per play and 330.1 yards per contest.

878 The number of rushing yards (878) gained from scrimmage by former Penn State Lion and seven-time NFL Pro Bowler Lenny Moore during his 1965 season with the Baltimore Colts. Moore was a five-time first-team All-Pro, and a 1975 NFL Hall of Fame selection.

879 The passing efficiency rating (87.9) for backup quarterback Daryll Clark during the 2006 PSU season. Clark found playing time in seven games and completed 14 of 27 passes for 116 yards.

880 The team leading number of rushing yards (880) for Tom Donchez in 1974. Donchez followed Heisman Trophy winner John Cappelletti in the Penn State backfield, carrying the football 195 times for a 4.5-yard average with seven touchdowns.

881 The number of passes (881) attempted by Todd Blackledge during a seven-year NFL career with the Kansas City Chiefs and the Pittsburgh Steelers. The Chiefs made Blackledge the seventh overall pick in the 1983 NFL draft after he won the Davey O'Brien Award given to the nation's top quarterback. The signal caller, however, ended his NFL career with more interceptions (38) than touchdowns (29), and never started more than 12 games in a season. Blackledge was part of a star-studded quarterback draft class that included John Elway, Jim Kelly, and Dan Marino.

The overall draft pick number and year (8, '82) in which Penn State offensive guard Mike Munchak was selected by the Houston Oilers with the eighth overall pick in the 1982 NFL draft. The former Business Logistics major went on to enjoy so much success that he was inducted into the Football Hall of Fame in 2001.

The number of kickoff return yards (883) compiled by the 2007 Nittany Lions. Derrick Williams was a star member of the Penn State special teams with 13 kickoff returns for 237 yards.

The total number of rushing yards (884) for Dave McNaughton during the 1965 season. McNaughton carried the football 193 times with a 4.6-yard average and seven touchdowns for the inconsistent Nittany Lions, who never won more than two straight games all season, finishing with a 5-5 mark.

The AP ranking and year (#8, '85) when Penn State played Alabama on October 12, 1985. 'Bama came into the game ranked #10, and in a tightly contested game, the Lions prevailed 19-17 in front of the home crowd.

The number of offensive plays (886) run by Penn State's opponents during the 2007 season. The Nittany Lion offense ran 943 plays, averaged a yard more per play (5.5) than opponents, and racked up 400.1 total yards per contest.

The number of wins and year (8, '87) Penn State posted eight victories during the 1987 season and earned an invite to play Clemson in the Citrus Bowl. Unfortunately, the Nittany Lions lost in Orlando by a score of 35-10, and closed out the season with an 8-4 record.

888 The area code (888) for purchasing a jersey of your favorite Penn State player. You can order customized, officially licensed PSU jerseys and other essential gear for tailgating by calling 1 (888) 237-1946.

889 The career record for average yards-per-attempt (8.89) set by Mike McQueary from 1994-97. McQueary completed 171 of 307 passes, good for 2,730 yards and 22 touchdowns with only 11 interceptions. He also set the school record for passing efficiency (145.57).

890 The number of rushing yards gained per game (89.0) by former Penn State Lion Franco Harris during his 1975 NFL season with the Steelers. During his 13-year NFL career, Harris finished with an average of 70.1 yards gained per game.

891 The month and year (8, '91) Penn State played Georgia Tech at Giants Stadium in East Rutherford, NJ during the annual Kickoff Classic. PSU came into the game ranked #7. After beating the Yellow Jackets 34-22, the Lions moved up to #5 the next week.

892 The number of rushing attempts (892) by former Lion Larry Johnson during his first four seasons in the NFL. Johnson rushed for over 4,200 yards from 2003-06 with the Kansas City Chiefs.

893 The passing efficiency rating (89.3) of Akron during Penn State's 34-16 win over the Zips on September 2, 2006. The Nittany Lions' first game of the 2006 season saw PSU's defense pick off two Akron passes.

894 The month and year (8, '94) that the Lions opened fall camp and prepared for the biggest rip-off in NCAA football history. As most PSU fans remember, Paterno led Penn State to an undefeated season at 12-0 and a Rose Bowl victory over Oregon 38-20. But after Nebraska also finished undefeated, the pollsters handed the Cornhuskers the national title and a #2 ranking to the Lions.

895 The red zone success percentage (89.5) for Penn State's offense going into its 2007 season finale with Texas A&M in the Alamo Bowl. The Nittany Lions converted on a Big Ten league leading 51 of 57 attempts inside the 20-yard line during the regular season.

896 The month and year (8, '96) Penn State opened its season against the #7 USC Trojans during the Kickoff Classic in East Rutherford, NJ. The #11 Lions sent USC back to California with a 24-7 beating. Based on this win, Penn State jumped to #7 in the polls the following week.

897 The day and year (8, '97) in November when the Nittany Lions suffered their first loss of the season at the claws of the Michigan Wolverines. Penn State started the season ranked #1 in the AP poll, but eventually ended up outside the Top 10.

898 The number of punt yards (898) for quarterback/punter/halfback Don Bailey in 1954. Bailey used his athletic ability to run head coach Rip Engle's option offense for the first time, and he also put up adequate passing totals with 393 yards, five touchdowns, and just two interceptions. He punted the football 26 times for a 34.5-yard average.

899 The number of passing yards (899) piled up by Jeff Hostetler during his final professional season with the Washington Redskins in 1997. The signal caller also led the New York Giants to victory in Super Bowl XXV. Hostetler played one year at Penn State before transferring to West Virginia after losing the quarterback competition to Todd Blackledge.

900 The number of times (900) running back Fran Rogel carried the football during his eight- year NFL career with the Pittsburgh Steelers. Rogel's best season came in 1955, when the multipurpose back rushed for 588 yards and a pair of touchdowns, and caught 24 passes for 222 yards. He made the Pro Bowl one season later and finished his career with 3,271 rushing yards and 17 rushing touchdowns. Rogel crossed the goal line on the ground 15 times as a Nittany Lion, rushing for 1,496 yards from 1947-49.

Penn State All-American Linebackers

- Andre Collins, 1989
- Brandon Short, 1999
- Bruce Clark, 1978, 1979
- Charlie Zapiec, 1971
- Dan Connor, 2006, 2007
- Dennis Onkotz, 1968, 1969
- Ed O'Neil, 1973
- Greg Buttle, 1975
- Jack Ham, 1970
- John Skorupan, 1972
- Kurt Allerman, 1976
- LaVar Arrington, 1998, 1999
- Paul Posluszny, 2005, 2006
- Shane Conlan, 1985, 1986

"The name ties in with the tradition that was established, and has been carried forward by so many football players."

—former defensive coordinator Jerry Sandusky to
The Daily Collegian in September 2000

Chapter Ten

Linebacker U's Never-Ending Story

Penn State is a world renowned research university. It boasts one of the nation's top business schools, a diverse student body, and is situated in a cookie cutter region where rolling countryside meets urban sprawl.

Yet, more than anything, Penn State is known for its linebackers, hence the university's well known nickname: Linebacker U.

The graduating class is as long as it is decorated. Most recently, tackling machines Dan Connor and Paul Posluszny have each been recognized as a first team All-American and the program's most frequent tackler—a distinction first held by Posluszny and then passed on to Connor during the 2007 season.

The square shouldered duo ended up in the same place at the ball carrier, but took very different routes in awakening the program from almost a decade of playmaking slumber. Connor avoided blockers with instincts and raw athleticism, while Posluszny took them head on with success, and found the ball carrier at the bottom of an all-out explosion.

The star-studded list of famous 'backers extends longer than the line at the Waffle House on a weekend morning (really, really long). LaVar Arrington was a two-time All-American with a vertical leap on full display during a highlight reel play against Illinois in 1998. Brandon Short was the substance to Arrington's style, manning the middle of Penn State's defense for three of his four seasons. Brian Gelzheiser and Mark D'Onofrio were steady stalwarts, while Andre Collins, Trey Bauer, and Shane Conlan were All-Americans and national champions.

Greg Buttle recorded 165 tackles in 1974, and Kurt Allerman joined him in the society of first team All-Americans. The list goes on to include another first team All-American (Ed O'Neil), and two members of the College Football Hall of Fame (Jack Ham and Dennis Onkotz).

That list, spanning the late 1960s and early 1970s with Ham and Onkotz, up until present day with the recently graduated Connor and new leader Sean Lee, has been a major part of Penn State's proud football history.

Almost like clockwork, Penn State approaches each season with simple threads bearing no names, black cleats, and amply-skilled linebackers. Success is built on a defensive approach that highlights the group's playmaking ability, and a ball controlled offense takes advantage of its opportunistic linebacker brethren.

It is also a matter of pride and purpose that drives each group of Nittany Lion linebackers.

"It's a huge thing for us just because we know all the great guys who have come before us, and to not try our hardest would be a disservice to them," Posluszny told *The Daily Collegian* prior to his junior season. "If we didn't try to uphold that, then we would be stamping on the tradition that is Penn State."

Upholding tradition. Penn State hasn't been college football's linebacker haven for nearly 40 years by accident. It has grown through a legacy of family and success and has shaped its brand with a slogan that is more than marketing.

Posluszny, Arrington, Collins, and Conlan have all followed Linebacker U's main mantra. *I play for those who came before me.*

That was a good idea, because they were all damn good.

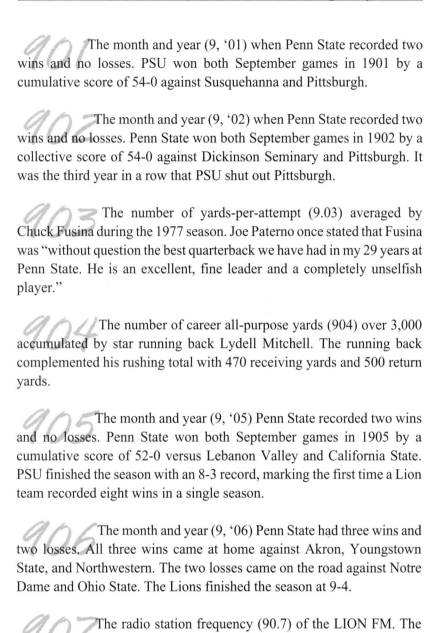

The month and year (9, '01) when Penn State recorded two wins and no losses. PSU won both September games in 1901 by a cumulative score of 54-0 against Susquehanna and Pittsburgh.

The month and year (9, '02) when Penn State recorded two wins and no losses. Penn State won both September games in 1902 by a collective score of 54-0 against Dickinson Seminary and Pittsburgh. It was the third year in a row that PSU shut out Pittsburgh.

The number of yards-per-attempt (9.03) averaged by Chuck Fusina during the 1977 season. Joe Paterno once stated that Fusina was "without question the best quarterback we have had in my 29 years at Penn State. He is an excellent, fine leader and a completely unselfish player."

The number of career all-purpose yards (904) over 3,000 accumulated by star running back Lydell Mitchell. The running back complemented his rushing total with 470 receiving yards and 500 return yards.

The month and year (9, '05) Penn State recorded two wins and no losses. Penn State won both September games in 1905 by a cumulative score of 52-0 versus Lebanon Valley and California State. PSU finished the season with an 8-3 record, marking the first time a Lion team recorded eight wins in a single season.

The month and year (9, '06) Penn State had three wins and two losses. All three wins came at home against Akron, Youngstown State, and Northwestern. The two losses came on the road against Notre Dame and Ohio State. The Lions finished the season at 9-4.

The radio station frequency (90.7) of the LION FM. The soundtrack to Penn State is a student run college radio station that transmits to a potential audience of over 125,000 listeners. In 1999, students at the LION began broadcasting Penn State Football.

The number of plays (908) the Penn State offense ran with Kareem McKenzie lined up at offensive tackle in 1999. McKenzie was a first-team All-Big Ten selection in his junior season with 85 pancake blocks as the team generated 5,014 yards. The three-time All-Big Ten selection was chosen in the third round of the 2001 NFL draft by the New York Jets.

The day and year (9, '09) in October when Penn State traveled to Wilkes-Barre, PA to take on the Carlisle Indian team. The game ended in an 8-8 tie. Bill Hollenback's squad also tied Penn later that year en route to a 5-0-2 record.

The month and year (9, '10) Head Coach Jack Hollenback opened fall training in preparation for Penn State's October 1 meeting with the Harrisburg Athletic Club. The Nittany Lions won the contest 58-0 and gave their new coach a 5-2-1 record.

The number of fans (911) over 40,000 that witnessed Joe Paterno's first victory as head coach, a 15-7 triumph over Maryland on September 17, 1966. The team presented Paterno with the game ball for the first of two times in his coaching career.

The day and year (9, '12) in November when Penn State hosted Villanova at New Beaver Field in State College. The Lions won the contest 71-0 en route to an undefeated 8-0 record. Only one team scored on PSU that year as the Nittany Lions outscored their opponents 285-6.

The number of passing yards (913) for two-way star Rich Lucas during the 1959 season. Lucas punted 20 times for a 34.0 yard average and returned 5 interceptions for 114 yards. Lucas won the Maxwell Award, was named a first-team All-American, and finished second in the 1959 Heisman Trophy balloting.

The career touchdown passing percentage (9.14) posted by Elwood Petchel. The true triple threat stood only 5' 8" and weighed just 145 pounds, but his determination and game smarts led to a 117.3 career passing efficiency. He threw a 30-yard touchdown pass in his first game back from World War II in 1946.

The month and year (9, '15) Penn State kicked off the season with a 26-0 win over Westminster. PSU started the year with five straight wins before tapering off and completing the season with a 7-2 record for head coach Dick Harlow.

The month and year (9, '16) the Nittany Lions started their campaign with a 27-0 win over Susquehanna at New Beaver Field. Penn State tailored four more shutouts that year as they completed their season with an 8-2 record.

The single game completion percentage record (91.7) set by Pete Liske in a 17-7 victory at Oregon in 1963. Liske completed 87 of 161 passes for 1,117 yards, 10 touchdowns and five interceptions in his second consecutive season as the starting quarterback.

The number of total tackles (918) credited to the Penn State defense over the course of the 2005 season. Paul Posluszny's 116 tackles bested the safety duo of Chris Harrell (88) and Calvin Lowry (79).

The month and year (9, '19) the *New York Times* reported Penn State would return 35 lettermen for the upcoming season. Practice opened on September 6 under the direction of Dick Harlow and freshman coach Dutch Herman.

The number of games and year (9, '20) for Penn State in the 1920 season. The Nittany Lions won their first seven games, but settled for ties during their final contests of the season and finished with a 7-0-2 record.

The number of times and year (9, '21) Penn State held its opponents to seven points or fewer nine times during 1921. The Nittany Lions outscored their opponents 251-56 en route to an 8-0-2 record that season.

The number of rushing yards (922) gained by Curt Warner during his 1980 sophomore season. Warner averaged 4.7 yards per carry and scored six rushing touchdowns on his way to legendary status.

The extra point accuracy percentage (92.3) for Ben Pollock during the 1937 season. Pollock was the first player to specialize in placekicking at Penn State when he moved from offensive guard to handle kicking duties as a sophomore—but he didn't play enough that season to earn a letter under the eligibility rules.

The month and year (9, '24) Penn State opened its season against Lebanon Valley at New Beaver Field. The Nittany Lions won their season opener 47-3 and finished the season with a 6-3-1 record on the year.

The combined number of career kickoff return yards and touchdowns (925) totaled by Curt Warner. He returned kicks for a total of 922 yards and 3 touchdowns. Warner put the Penn State offense in prime field position, and then took advantage of that position with grinding 4-yard runs and plenty of 20-yard sprints. He returned 32 career kickoffs for a 28.8 yard average.

The day and year (9, '26) in October when the Nittany Lions hosted Marietta at New Beaver Field. Penn State won the game 48-6 for its third straight victory up to that point of the season—but it closed out the year at 5-4.

The month and year (9, '27) Penn State opened its season with a 27-0 win over Lebanon Valley in State College. This was Penn State's only September game in a season that saw the Lions go 6-2-1 for Coach Hugo Bezdek.

The number of games and year (9, '28) for Penn State in the 1928 season. Penn State hosted five games that year and made trips to in-state rivals Penn, Pitt, and Lafayette. Even the Notre Dame game was played in Philly.

The day and year (9, '29) in November when Penn State traveled to Franklin Field in Philadelphia to play in-state rival Penn. PSU won the game 19-7—its last win of the year before closing out with two losses and finishing with a 6-3 record.

The month and year (9, '30) when Bob Higgins made his head coaching debut at PSU. The Nittany Lions took on Niagara at home, winning 31-14. Higgins earned All-American honors as a player at Penn State in 1915, then after serving in the military during World War I, he earned All-American honors a second time in 1919.

The number of tackles (931) credited to the Penn State defense during the 2007 season. Dan Connor and Sean Lee outdistanced their fellow teammates with 145 and 138 total tackles respectively.

The number of typed words (932) in Andy Baggot's September 19, 2001 *Wisconsin State Journal* article titled *He's College Football—Penn State Coach Joe Paterno is One Win Away From Tying the Division I-A Record.*

The time left in the second quarter in minutes and seconds (9:33) when Zack Mills scored on an eight yard run against Southern Miss to give the Lions a 17-7 lead. PSU won the November 3, 2001 game 38-20. The touchdown essentially broke the game open.

The cost in dollars and cents ($9.34) for a Penn State alumni window decal at NittanyOutlet.com. The website offers deals on everything from shirts and caps to key chains and umbrellas. Their motto: Everything Penn State.

The combined number of games played and sacks (93.5) for defensive tackle Pete Kugler during a decorated NFL career with the San Francisco 49ers. He posted 12.5 sacks in 81 games. Kugler played in three Super Bowls (1982, 1989, and 1990) after a solid collegiate career on a defensive line that included Bruce Clark, Matt Millen, and Larry Kubin.

The number of rushing yards (936) gained by West Virginia's Major Harris during his junior season. The year before, Penn State will remember him for dismantling its defense in a 51-30 beating. Harris outgained the entire Penn State team, 301-292 yards.

The number of passing yards (937) totaled by Tony Rados during the 1952 season. Rados completed 93 of 186 passes with eight touchdowns, and the next season he was good for 1,025 yards and eight scores. Penn State finished 7-2-1 in 1952, and then completed the 1953 season with a 6-3 record.

The average number of rushing yards (93.8) the Penn State defense surrendered per contest in 2007. The Nittany Lions front seven dominated the trenches, holding opponents to just 2.7 yards per rush attempt. On the flip side, Penn State's rushing offense churned out 193.8 yards per game.

The month and year (9, '39) Penn State opened up preseason workouts to prepare for the upcoming season. The 1939 squad beat Pitt for the first time in 20 years, prompting President Hetzel to declare the following Monday a holiday for students.

The number of receiving yards (940) tight end Kyle Brady compiled throughout his collegiate career. The big man with the soft hands caught 76 passes with nine touchdowns and 12.4 yards per catch.

The number of receiving yards (941) amassed by wide receiver Michael Timpson during his 1994 season with the New England Patriots. Timpson, a former Nittany Lion, made 74 of his 300 career receptions that season, and scored three of his 12 touchdowns.

The month and year (9, '42) *The Daily Collegian* reported that Penn State's team would be primarily made up of freshman after losing 27 members of the previous year's varsity squad. Potentially a problem, yes, but in the end, the squad posted a 6-1-1 record.

The number of yards (943) Tom Sherman threw for during the 1966 season. Sherman threw six touchdown passes, but more than doubled that with 13 scoring tosses one year later. The signal caller threw for 1,616 yards in 1967.

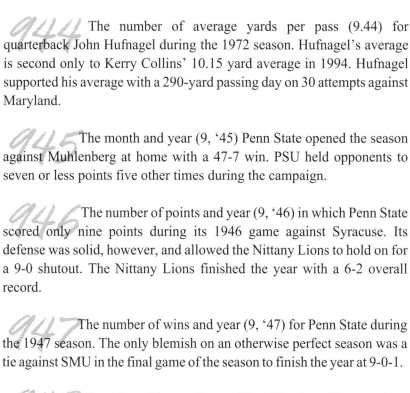

944 The number of average yards per pass (9.44) for quarterback John Hufnagel during the 1972 season. Hufnagel's average is second only to Kerry Collins' 10.15 yard average in 1994. Hufnagel supported his average with a 290-yard passing day on 30 attempts against Maryland.

945 The month and year (9, '45) Penn State opened the season against Muhlenberg at home with a 47-7 win. PSU held opponents to seven or less points five other times during the campaign.

946 The number of points and year (9, '46) in which Penn State scored only nine points during its 1946 game against Syracuse. Its defense was solid, however, and allowed the Nittany Lions to hold on for a 9-0 shutout. The Nittany Lions finished the year with a 6-2 overall record.

947 The number of wins and year (9, '47) for Penn State during the 1947 season. The only blemish on an otherwise perfect season was a tie against SMU in the final game of the season to finish the year at 9-0-1.

948 The AP ranking and year (#9, '48) when #9 Penn State played West Virginia. The Lions won the game 37-7 and went on to finish the season 7-1-1. The Lions only loss of the season was a bitter 7-0 defeat at the hands of rival Pitt that dropped them to #18 in the rankings.

949 TThe month and year (9, '49) Penn State opened its season with a 27-6 loss to Villanova at home. Penn State started the year with two losses, but was able to put a 5-4 winning record together by season's end.

950 The number of points scored (950) by PSU opponents from 1940-50. Penn State recorded a 67-23-6 record during this time frame under coaches Bob Higgins, Joe Bedenk, and Rip Engle.

951 The month and year (9, '51) that Penn State recorded a 40-34 win over Boston University. The September 29, 1951 meeting was PSU's only September game that year and was played in front of 15,536 fans.

The month and year (9, '52) Penn State recorded a 20-13 win over Temple and a 20-20 tie with Purdue. The Lions finished the season with a 7-2-1 record after a 17-0 victory over Pitt on November 22 in front of 53,766 fans.

The month and year (9, '53) Penn State lost at Wisconsin 20-0 in front of 49,000 Badger fans. The September 26 meeting was the only September game for the Lions that year. Penn State finished the season 6-3.

The average number of all-purpose yards-per-game (95.4) gained by Derrick Williams during the 2005 season. Williams totaled 105 yards rushing, 289 yards receiving, and 274 kickoff return yards during the year. The Washington D.C. native was an All-*USA Today* selection, All-Metro choice by the *Washington Post*, and a *Parade Magazine* All-American all-purpose player in high school.

The quarterback efficiency rating (95.5) for backup Daryll Clark against Temple in 2006. Clark finished the season with 116 yards on 14 of 27 passing.

The number of total offensive yards (956) Gary Wydman racked up over the course of the 1964 campaign. Wydman was a part of the action during 248 plays, including two scoring snaps, for the Nittany Lions.

The month and year (9, '57) the Lions beat the Penn Quakers 19-14 in front of 21,150 fans. The September 28, 1957 game was Penn State's only September game of the year. PSU finished the campaign at 6-3.

The number of average all-purpose yards per game (95.8) for Michigan Wolverine and All-American wide receiver David Terrell during the 1999 season. Before Terrell made his way to Ann Arbor, he won the fastest 40 yard dash award at the Penn State summer football camp with a time of 4.31 seconds.

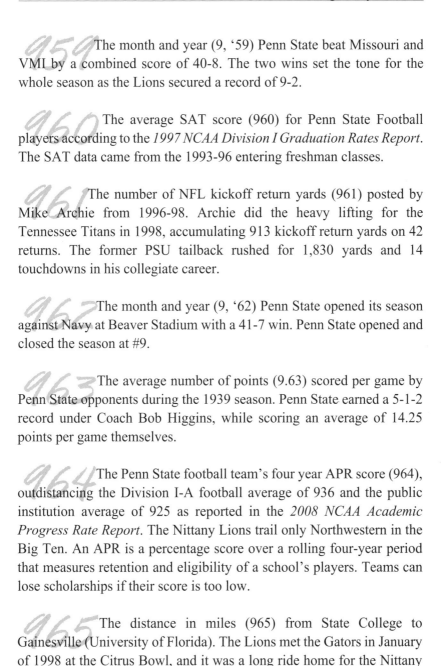

The month and year (9, '59) Penn State beat Missouri and VMI by a combined score of 40-8. The two wins set the tone for the whole season as the Lions secured a record of 9-2.

The average SAT score (960) for Penn State Football players according to the *1997 NCAA Division I Graduation Rates Report*. The SAT data came from the 1993-96 entering freshman classes.

The number of NFL kickoff return yards (961) posted by Mike Archie from 1996-98. Archie did the heavy lifting for the Tennessee Titans in 1998, accumulating 913 kickoff return yards on 42 returns. The former PSU tailback rushed for 1,830 yards and 14 touchdowns in his collegiate career.

The month and year (9, '62) Penn State opened its season against Navy at Beaver Stadium with a 41-7 win. Penn State opened and closed the season at #9.

The average number of points (9.63) scored per game by Penn State opponents during the 1939 season. Penn State earned a 5-1-2 record under Coach Bob Higgins, while scoring an average of 14.25 points per game themselves.

The Penn State football team's four year APR score (964), outdistancing the Division I-A football average of 936 and the public institution average of 925 as reported in the *2008 NCAA Academic Progress Rate Report*. The Nittany Lions trail only Northwestern in the Big Ten. An APR is a percentage score over a rolling four-year period that measures retention and eligibility of a school's players. Teams can lose scholarships if their score is too low.

The distance in miles (965) from State College to Gainesville (University of Florida). The Lions met the Gators in January of 1998 at the Citrus Bowl, and it was a long ride home for the Nittany Lions after a 21-6 defeat.

The month and year (9, '66) Joe Pa took over as the head coach at Penn State. The Lions played two games in September of 1966; a

15-7 win over Maryland and a 42-8 loss at #1 Michigan State in East Lansing.

The number of times and year (9, '67) Penn State won or tied for Joe Paterno's first winning season at the helm. The club went 8-2-1 overall in 1967, but most importantly the club was well on its way to national prominence under the Brooklyn bred football mind.

Ohio State and USC both won nine games during the 1968 season (9, '68)—pretty impressive, until you consider that PSU was 11-0 that season. And yet, somehow, both the Buckeyes and Trojans were ranked ahead of the Nittany Lions at season's end.

The month and year (9, '69) Penn State opened its second consecutive undefeated season with a 45-22 victory at Navy. Although the Nittany Lions went unbeaten, President Richard Nixon awarded the national title to Texas after the Longhorns beat Arkansas on December 6, 1969.

The number of times and year (9, '71) Penn State scored 30 or more points against its opponents during the 1971 regular season, including a 30-6 victory over the Texas Longhorns in the Cotton Bowl to finish at 11-1.

The number of times and year (9, '71) Penn State scored 30 or more points against their opponents during the 1971 regular season, including a 30-6 victory over the Texas Longhorns in the Cotton Bowl to finish at 11-1.

The number of total tackles (972) credited to the Penn State defense during the 2003 season. Gino Capone recorded an even 100 tackles and Deryck Tolles added 75 total stops.

The number of receiving yards (973) totaled during Freddie Scott's 47-catch 1994 season. Scott played in Bobby Engram's shadow, but reached the end zone two more times and averaged a lofty 20.7 yards per reception.

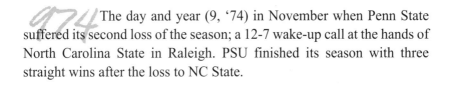

The day and year (9, '74) in November when Penn State suffered its second loss of the season; a 12-7 wake-up call at the hands of North Carolina State in Raleigh. PSU finished its season with three straight wins after the loss to NC State.

The number of wins and year (9, '75) for Penn State during the 1975 season. The Lions started the year at #6 and finished at #10 in both the AP and Coaches polls after posting a 9-3 record.

The number of typed words (976) by *Minneapolis Star Tribune*'s Mark Craig in his 2001 Big Ten Football review published on August 30. The writer calls Joe Pa, "feisty, yet funny and clever."

The number of yards (977) wide receiver O.J. McDuffie amassed during his 1992 senior season. McDuffie left Penn State with his name atop 15 school receiving, return, and all-purpose yardage records.

The first three digits (978) in the ISBN number for *Game Day: Penn State Football* by *Athlon Sports* and *Triumph Books*. Order your copy at any online bookstore by using the full ISBN: 978-1-60078-014-1.

The number of points and year (9, '79) Penn State scored against #15 Tulane in the 1979 Liberty Bowl. The Lions won the contest 9-6 and finished the year at 8-4 with a Coaches ranking of #18 and an AP ranking of #20.

The round and year (9, '80) Penn State wide receiver Tom Donovan was selected by the Kansas City Chiefs in the 1980 NFL draft, making him the #230 overall pick. The only Nittany Lion to go in the first round was defensive tackle Bruce Clark, who was selected by the Green Bay Packers as the fourth overall pick.

The AP preseason ranking prior to the 1981 season (#9, '81) for Penn State. The Nittany Lions only improved on that ranking as they stomped Cincinnati in the season opener, 52-0. The Lions went on to post a 10-2 record and a #3 ranking.

The AP ranking and year (#9, '82) for Penn State halfway through the 1982 season before it caught fire and ran off six straight victories. Penn State finished the year at 11-1 and ended the season with a Sugar Bowl win over Georgia and a #1 ranking.

The number of Penn State players (9, '83) who were selected in the 1983 NFL draft. Curt Warner was the first Penn State player picked and went to the Seattle Seahawks as the #3 overall pick in the draft.

The approximate number of miles (984) between HOK Sports' Kansas City, Missouri office and Penn State's campus in University Park, PA. Former Nittany Lion linebacker Scott Radecic—an Academic All-American at Penn State—is a senior principal at the sports architecture firm responsible for the expansion of Beaver Stadium. Radecic made 48 solo stops and 23 assisted tackles during Penn State's 1982 national championship season.

The number of rushing yards (985) compiled by Seattle Seahawks running back Curt Warner during the 1987 season. Warner continued the positive momentum from the previous campaign, when he rushed for a career best 1,481 yards and 13 touchdowns.

The number of times and year (9, '86) Penn State scored 20 or more points en route to a perfect 12-0 season and a national championship. The Nittany Lions outscored their opponents 340-133 that season.

The number of team leading receiving yards (987) compiled by Bobby Engram on a team best 64 catches for the Chicago Bears during the 1998 season. Engram started his professional career in the Windy City after amassing 4,043 all-purpose yards at Penn State, joining Curt Warner and Blair Thomas in the select 4,000-yard club.

The average number of rushing yards per game (98.8) collected by Rodney Kinlaw during the 2007 season. Kinlaw ran for 1,186 yards — the 10th best yardage tally by any PSU running back to that date — in 12 games for the Nittany Lions.

989 The name of the video game production company (989 Sports) responsible for placing Larry Johnson on the cover of NCAA Gamebreaker 2004. Johnson was the first Penn State player to be highlighted on the cover of a video game in a Nittany Lion uniform.

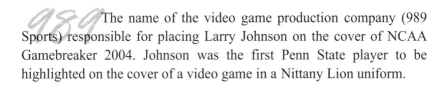 **990** The radio station frequency (990) of WNTP AM out of Philadelphia that carries Penn State football. WNTP AM airs each regular season and bowl game with play-by-play announcer Steve Jones and Jack Ham on the call. The radio station also carries the annual Blue-White game in April.

991 The number of passing yards (991) John Andress accumulated in 1975. Andress completed 71 of 149 passes for the Nittany Lions, who finished a 9-3 season with a loss to Alabama in the Sugar Bowl. The signal caller completed 8 of 14 passes for 57 yards in that final defeat.

992 The number of receiving yards (992) recorded by John Gilmore during his brief two-year high school career at Wilson High School in West Lawn, PA. Gilmore caught 33 passes for 667 yards and eight touchdowns during his senior campaign. Gilmore's brother Pete was a freshman running back at Penn State during his senior season.

993 The number of points (993) Penn State logged in the 2003 NACDA Directors' Cup final standings. In a points-based tally that rates the success of men's and women's athletic programs at universities nationwide, the Nittany Lions finished fifth behind Stanford, Texas, and Big Ten brethren Ohio State and Michigan. The Penn State football team placed 39th with 34 points.

994 The AP ranking and year (9, '94) for Penn State at the beginning of the 1994 season. The Lions continued to improve on that ranking as the season continued and went on to an undefeated season. Unfortunately, the Lions received the AP #2 ranking at the end of the season behind Nebraska.

995 The overall draft pick and year (9, '95) Penn State tight end Kyle Brady was selected by the New York Jets in the 1995 NFL draft.

The #1 overall pick that year was Penn State running back Ki-Jana Carter, who was chosen by the Cincinnati Bengals.

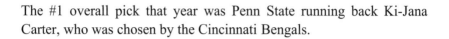The pick number and year (9, '96) Penn State running back Mike Archie was selected by the Houston Oilers in round seven of the 1996 NFL draft. He was the #218 overall pick, and nine of his Nittany Lions' teammates are on the list of players drafted ahead of him.

The number of wins and year (9, '97) for Penn State in the 1997 season. The Lions began the year ranked #1, but finished the season with a 9-3 record and a #16 ranking.

The number of wins and year (9, '98) for Penn State in the 1998 season. The Lions earned an invite to the Outback Bowl and beat Kentucky 26-14 in front of 66,005 fans.

The number of consecutive wins and year (9, '99) Penn State started with in the 1999 season. The team also scored 27 or more points nine times that season. Unfortunately, the team ended the campaign with three consecutive defeats before notching a 24-0 win over Texas A&M in the Alamo Bowl. PSU was #11 in the final AP poll with a final record of 10-3.

The single season receiving yardage barrier (1,000) only Bobby Engram has managed to break throughout the program's history. The wide receiver totaled 1,084 yards on 63 catches for the high powered Nittany Lions offense in 1995.

Bibliography

Words sustain our being, encapsulate our dreams, wipe away—and sadly at times— perpetuate our tears. Words are the strongest form of emotion—they detail our daily lives and record history for the generations that come after us.

For the purpose of this historical dissertation, words—and numbers—tie together a program's highs and lows for a legacy of Penn Staters. Those facts were found in many of the university's media guides and at the official online home of Nittany Lion football.

This bibliography practically begins and ends at www.gopsusports.com. The football sub-page features team records, All-Americans, NFL stars, bowl records and game highlights, and all-time polls. The online record book is chalk full of offensive and defensive stand-outs and the statistical portion looks at game and season numbers as far back as 1997.

The way-back machine brought me to a true Penn State historian— acclaimed author Louis Prato. His 600-plus page guide to Penn State football was a life saver. "The Penn State Football Encyclopedia" is officially licensed and endorsed by the university and features information about the Rip Engle era and the program as far back as the test of time. All lettermen are discussed—briefly in some cases, and much more extensively in others. Louis Prato's due diligence provided an excellent reference guide for my interpretation of Penn State pigskin history.

The best of the rest is listed below. A writer is only as good as his research—and not surprisingly—Penn State football was high up on every search engine and had many articles, books, and reference guides floating in the published world.

The Penn State Football Encyclopedia. Louis Prato. Champaign, Illinois: Sports Publishing, Inc., 1998.

The Night College Football Went to Hell. Michael Weinreb. ESPN.com.

Johnson gains 327 yards, breaks 2 Penn State records in 58-25 victory. Ray Fittipaldo. Pittsburgh Post-Gazette. November 17, 2002.

Robinson Finds His Comfort Zone. Joe LaPointe. New York Times. November 18, 2005.

Joe Paterno: Football My Way. Mervin D. Hyman and Gordon S. White. Macmillian Publishing Company, 1978.

Bringing Back Linebacker U. Justin Kunkel. The Daily Collegian. April 22, 2005.

johncappelletti73heisman.com

www.gopsusports.com

Index

Special Thanks

The three of us—Dan, David, and Marc—continue to be supported by an outstanding team of people who have been diligent and patient with us, and at the same time, dedicated to the success of our Sports by the Numbers™ franchise.

Thank you to our publisher who makes all this possible, Theodore P. "Ted" Savas, and the fine team of professionals he assembled in California: Sarah, Veronica, Tammy, Alex, Val, Jim, and Lee.

We have many friends, colleagues, and family members-too many to list here-who continue to show their support for us daily. Often that support comes by staying out of our way as we frantically rush to meet deadlines-but more frequently still it comes in the form of an encouraging word, helping us out at book signings and other events, or simply letting us kick around new ideas and asking for advice when they know, in the end, we are going to end up doing exactly what we want anyway.

You guys know who you are—so thanks for everything.

For our past and present friends at Penn State: Cathy Watson, Dr. Eunice Askov, Dr. Ian Baptiste, Dr. Gary Kuhne, Dr. Michael Moore, Dr. Jaime M. Fenton, and Dr. Derek Mulenga. Thank you for making the World Campus a great PSU experience.

Our parents are our biggest fans: Bill and Dorthe Brush, Larry and Connie Horne, and Richard and Deanna Maxwell.

Well, almost.

The ones who make sense out of this crazy world for us: Paulina, Lisa, and Christine.

Daniel J. Brush, David Horne, Marc CB Maxwell
Norman, Oklahoma
June 1, 2009